The Fire Horse

History of the horse-drawn Fire Engine

Gloria Austin's Collection of Books

Gloria Austin is an award winning preservationist, carriage collector, and holds many championship titles.

www.GloriaAustin.com

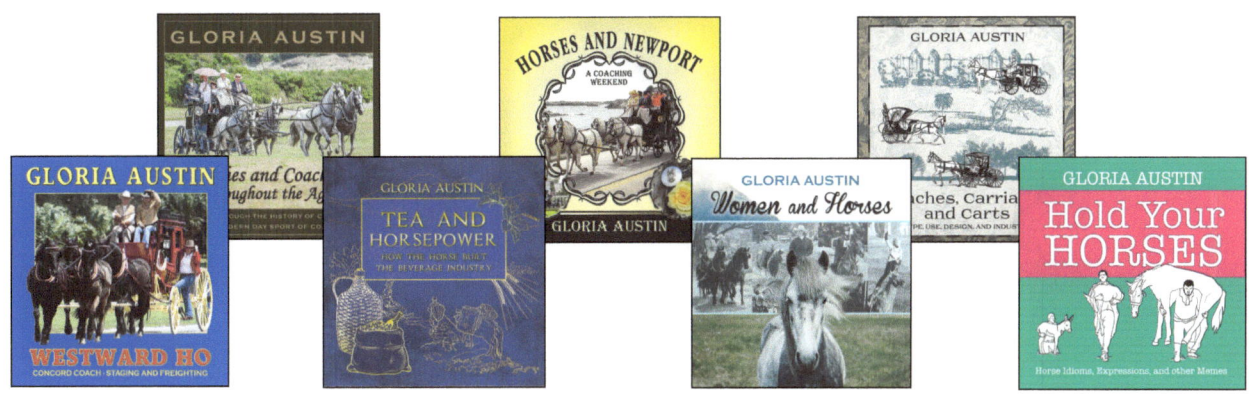

ENJOY OUR OTHER BOOKS

- The Brewster Story
- Carriage Lamps
- Gloria Austin's Carriage Collection
- A Glossary of Harness Parts
- Equine Elegance
- The Fire Horse
- Horse Basics 101
- Westward Ho!

- The Unsung Heros of World War One
- The Horse, History, and Human Culture
- Horse Symbolism
- Horses of the Americas
- A Drive Through Time
- The Medieval Horse
- Speak Your Horse's Language

- Tea: Steeped in Tradition
- Woman and Horses
- The Golden Carriage and the House of Hapsburg
- Horses and Newport
- A Cookbook for Horse Lovers
- Dance! To Improve Riding and Driving

Brought To You By The Equine Heritage Institute

The Fire Horse
By: Gloria Austin President of Equine Heritage Institute, Inc. (EHI)

2nd Edition 2023
First Published 2018
Copyright © 2023 by Equine Heritage Institute, Inc.

All rights reserved. No part of this publication may be reproduced, distributed, or transmitted in any form or by any means, including photocopying, recording, or other electronic or mechanical methods, without the prior written permission of the publisher, except in the case of brief quotations embodied in critical reviews, and certain other noncommercial uses permitted by copyright law. For permission requests, write to the publisher, addressed "Attention: Permissions Coordinator," at the address below.

Equine Heritage Institute, Inc.
3024 Marion County Road Weirsdale, FL 32195
Office: (352) 753-2826 Fax: (352) 753-6186

Ordering Information:
Quantity sales: Special discounts are available on quantity purchases by corporations, associations, and others. For details, contact the publisher at the address above.
ISBN: Print 978-1-951895-24-2

Cover:
Barney, Gene and Tom, Washington DC's last fire horses, on their 'last run'. and 1800's Antique Fireman Fire Department FDNY Certificate

Table of Contents

9   Introduction

11 **PART I –**
    HISTORIC FIRES
12 Rome 64 AD
13 London 1666
14 Boston 1760
15 New York 1835
16 Chicago 1871
17 Boston 1872
18 San Francisco 1906

21 **PART II –**
    THE DEVELOPMENT OF
    INSURANCE AND FIRE
    DEPARTMENTS
23 The First Systems of Fire
    Insurance & Fire Departments
24 The Early Development
    of Insurance and Firefighting
    in America

31 **PART III –**
    THE EVOLUTION OF
    FIREFIGHTING
    EQUIPMENT
33 Equipment and Methods for
    Fighting Fires

43 **PART IV –**
    THE FIRE HORSE SAVES
    THE DAY
45 The Need for Horses
47 Horse Drawn Vehicles
55 Harnesses and Other
    Equipment
59 Rules and Regulations
63 The Daily Routine
65 The Sound of the Alarm!
74 Types of Horses
76 Care and Training of Horses
86 Fire Horse Stories
99 Fire Horses - The Public
    Relations Team of the Fire
    Department
104 The End of an Era
105 Last Runs – A Sad Farewell

112 Conclusion
115 Sources
119 Image Sources

HISTORIC FIRES

- *587 BC – The destruction of the Temple and city of Jerusalem.* [170]

- *330 BC – Persepolis destroyed by fire after its capture by Alexander the Great.*
- *146 BC – Carthage was systematically burned down over 17 days by the Romans at the end of the Third Punic War*
- *64 – Great Fire of Rome, Italy.* [171]

SPECIAL THANKS TO

Mary Chris Foxworthy, Research Writer

Mary Chris' grandfather owned one of the last creameries in the United States that still used horse-drawn milk wagons. This sparked her life-long love affair with horses and passion for keeping horse history alive. After graduating from college with a degree in Food Science and Communications, Mary Chris bought her very first horse with her first paycheck. Since then, she has served on the board of various equine associations and held a judge's card in Carriage Driving. She is known for her work in the Gloria Austin Collection, and has published and presented numerous equine educational programs. She has written for several equine publications and won an award from American Horse Publications for one of her articles. Mary Chris is an active exhibitor in Carriage Driving and Dressage. Along with her husband, she enjoys spending time with their horses (two Morgans and a PRE), a bouncing Bearded Collie and two adult children and one grandchild.

With very special thanks to:

The Detroit Historical Society

Detroit Fire Legacy

Los Angeles Fire Department Historical Society

BROUGHT TO YOU BY

The books created by Equine Heritage Institute are designed to preserve the history and majesty of the horse. Our goal is to find, understand, and pass on the valuable data about equine use and its influence on humanity. The Equine Heritage Institute is a not for profit 501(c)(3) and 100% of all proceeds from the sale of books, services, and products support Equine Heritage Institute's mission.

To make a donation to EHI, please visit EHI-store.square.site/s/shop

A COPY OF THE OFFICIAL REGISTRATION AND FINANCIAL INFORMATION MAY BE OBTAINED FROM THE DIVISION OF CONSUMER SERVICES BY CALLING TOLL-FREE WITHIN THE STATE REGISTRATION DOES NOT IMPLY ENDORSEMENT, APPROVAL, OR RECOMMENDATION BY THE STATE. s. 496.411, F.S.

1-800-HELP-FLA (435-7352)   www.FloridaConsumerHelp.com

Introduction

Throughout history there have been many fires and many methods for putting out those fires. These "Great Fires" have several consistencies; the speed at which the fire spread, the difficulty in containing the fire and the struggle to extinguish the fire. Each fire brought changes in how cities were rebuilt from the ashes. Each fire also brought changes in firefighting methods. The growth of insurance companies and man's resistance to change is very much a part of the story of firefighting. For a brief 60 year period between the introduction of the external combustion steam engine and the internal combustion automotive engine that replaced it, the fire horse was the hero of fighting fires! Gloria's Carriage Collection at one time, had many pieces of firefighting equipment from the horse firefighting era. She was often called upon to discuss and present on this equipment. This precipitated the writing of this book. Mary Chris spent a great deal of time working with local fire houses countrywide, researching, fact checking and writing much of the information in this book. Her skills combined with Gloria's presentations and session notes brought forth a book filled with the honor, skill and dedication of the fire horse.

Print reads: "Insurance against Fire Only. Capital 500,000 Dolls" Fire fighters manning firehoses and pump wagons. Statue of a female figure standing on a pedestal emblazoned with a shield showing symbols of commerce, she is holding a pike on which is a banner that states "Indemnity"; at her feet is a large eagle.
Kneass, William, 1780-1840, engraver. [1]

- *79 – Lyon burned to ashes.*
- *406 – A great fire burns down much of Constantinople.*
- *532 – The Nika riots result in the destruction of much of Constantinople by fire.* [173]

- *798 – London nearly destroyed.*
- *847 – Borgo, Italy, the area around Saint Peter's Basilica in Rome, was devastated by fire.*
- *1041 – Fire destroys most of the old city of Bremen, Germany, including the cathedral.*
- *1046 – A fire in Hildesheim, Germany, destroys parts of the city, including the cathedral.*
- *1132 – In June, a huge fire in Hangzhou, China, destroyed 13,000 houses.*
- *1135 – Great Medieval London Fire of 1135. The first of the two Great Medieval Fires of London. This blaze was so severe that it destroyed most of the city between St Paul's and St Clement Danes in Westminster.*
- *1137 – A Great Fire in Hangzhou, China, destroyed 10,000 houses.*
- *1157 – First Fire of Lübeck, Germany, destroys the city.*

PART I - HISTORIC FIRES

Rome 64 AD

Rome fire [1a]

Cause: Although there were many Great Fires in ancient Rome, the fire of 64 is the best-known fire. There has been speculation that Nero started the fire of 64, so that he could clear out some valuable real estate to build a new palace. Nero used the fire to justify the persecution of the Christians since many blamed them for the fire. Once the fire started on the night of July 19th, in the shop district around the Circus Maximus, it spread quickly and burned Rome for 5 ½ days.

Firefighting: Fires in ancient Rome were a daily occurrence. In 22 BC, Augustus organised fire services in the 14 districts for administrative services. The "fire fighters" lived in barracks and thus provided 24-hour service. The Romans were famous for their hydraulics; the aqueducts were a great resource to fight fire. After the fire of 6 AD, Augustus established a corps of "vigiles" that became the model for our modern concept of civil protection. The brigade was overseen by an equestrian-level prefect on the lookout for arsonists and emergencies. The vigiles were expected to patrol the town at night with axes and buckets. When fires broke out, they also used hydraulic pumps for water. Men called Siphonarii were in charge of deploying pumps that could bring water in and douse a fire. According to Roman historian, Tacitus, in his book "The Annals" written in 116, fire brigades most likely did not contest the fire of 64 because they were likely told to stand down. After six days, the organized clearing of built-up areas brought the fire to a halt before it reached the Esquiline Hill. (cited from: https://www.forbes.com/sites/drsarahbond/2017/07/18/july-18-64-the-great-fire-of-nero-and-the-ancient-history-of-firefighting/#28ea02aa9544)

Damage: According to Tacitus, the Great Fire of 64 AD "… began in the Circus, where it adjoins the Palatine and Caelian hills. breaking out in shops and fanned by the wind, the inferno instantly grew and swept the whole length of the Circus. There were no walled mansions or temples, or any other obstructions, which could arrest it. First, the fire swept violently over the level spaces. Then it climbed the hills - but returned to ravage the lower ground again. It outstripped every counter-measure. The inhabitants of the city lived mostly in wooden houses and shacks and the ancient city's narrow winding streets and irregular blocks encouraged the progress of the flames. Of Rome's 14 districts only four remained intact. Three were leveled to the ground. The other 7 were reduced to a few scorched and mangled ruins." (cited from: http://www.eyewitnesstohistory.com/rome.htm)

Rebuild: After the fire, Nero began the biggest single building project in history. Materials and supplies were garnered from across the entire empire. A city made of marble and stone grew from the ashes. The redesign included wider streets, plenty of pedestrian arcades and ample supplies of water to extinguish any future fires..

London 1666

The Great Fire of London flattened four fifths of the city including St Paul's Cathedral. [1b]

Cause: On the evening of September 1, 1666,, the King's baker, Thomas Farrinor failed to properly extinguish his oven and went to bed. Sometime around midnight sparks from the smoldering embers ignited firewood lying beside the oven. Before long, his house was in flames. Farrinor managed to escape with his family and a servant out an upstairs window, but a bakery assistant died in the flames – the first victim. Sparks from Farrinor's bakery leapt across the street and set fire to straw and fodder in the stables of the Star Inn. From the Inn, the fire spread to Thames Street, where riverfront warehouses packed full with flammable materials such as tallow for candles, lamp oil, spirits, and coal, caught on fire or exploded, transforming the fire into an uncontrollable blaze. (cited from: https://www.history.com/this-day-in-history/great-fire-of-london-begins) After the fire, Farina continued to serve as the king's baker. He managed to escape blame due to widespread theories that the Fire was part of a Jesuit plot to assassinate the King.

Firefighting: In the beginning people attempted a bucket brigade to put out the fire, but as the fire spread rapidly, bucket-bearing locals abandoned efforts at firefighting and rushed home to evacuate their families and save their valuables. As the fire grew, city authorities struggled to tear down buildings and create a firebreak, but the flames repeatedly overtook them before they could complete their work. People fled into the Thames River dragging their possessions, and the homeless took refuge in the hills on the outskirts of London. Light from the Great Fire was reported to be seen 30 miles away. On September 5, the fire slackened, and on September 6 it was brought under control. That evening, flames again burst forth in the legal district but the explosion of buildings with gunpowder extinguished the flames. (cited from: https://www.history.com/this-day-in-history/great-fire-of-london-begins)

Damage: 13,200 houses, 87 churches (including old St. Paul's Cathedral), several hospitals, libraries and a prison, as well as 10,000 boats and barges on the river were all destroyed. (cited from: "Where Have All the Horses Gone", p.92) There were only 6 recorded deaths but the reason could be that the bodies were incinerated and, since the fire was in the slums, there were no records of inhabitants who lived there.

Rebuild: The Great Plague had swept through the city the previous summer. The fire, in a way, cleansed the city and paved the way for a rebuild. To prevent future fires, most new houses were built of brick or stone and separated by thicker walls. Narrow alleyways were forbidden and streets were made wider.

Boston 1760

Cause: Until the fire of 1760, the fire of 1711 had been called "The Great Fire". Other serious fires up to that time occurred in 1653, 1676, 1679, 1682, 1691 and 1753. Boston's location on a densely packed peninsula in a windy harbor meant that it had more blazes than any other colonial metropolis. The fire of 1760 was actually several fires. On March 17, a blaze damaged several buildings in the West End, including the wooden meeting house which stood on the current site of the Old West Church. On the following day a fire broke out in a building occupied by the Royal Artillery on Griffin's Wharf and soon spread to a quantity of gunpowder and weapons, causing an explosion that destroyed the building and injured 4 or 5 men. It's not clear what started any of the fires but the fact that buildings were mostly wood and many fires and chimneys were not attended and lighting was by candles, it's easy to understand how fires started and spread so rapidly.

The Angel of Death Flying Over the Great Boston Fire. Woodcut by Zechariah Fowle and Samuel Draper, 1760. [1c]

Firefighting: Volunteers and members of the Boston Fire Society joined the 'engine companies' with their hand-pumped 'fire engine' to combat the blaze. The wind-whipped blaze spread quickly to businesses and homes. The fire raged for ten hours. Hundreds of residents fled with no place to take refuge. Those who were ill were evacuated. David Perry, a sailor from Nova Scotia, recorded in his journal: "In spite of all we could do with the engines, it spread a great way down King's Street, and went across and laid all that part of the town in ashes, down to Fort Hill. We attended through the whole and assisted in carrying water to the engines." (cited from: https://www.massmoments.org/moment-details/boston-burns/submoment/boston-resolves-to-pay-firefighters.html)

Damage: 349 dwellings, stores, and shops were utterly consumed and one thousand people were left homeless. None were reported dead and only a few were injured. (cited from: http://www.kellscraft.com/GreatFireOfBoston/GreatFireofBostonCh02.html)

Rebuild: In order to prevent a similar disaster from occurring in the future, the Massachusetts legislature passed new laws and acts that improved fire safety standards in Boston. Any new building more than seven feet high that was made of wood would result in a fine, and a committee was appointed to re-lay the narrow streets of the burnt district. As a result of the new regulations, the homes that were rebuilt in the area were made of brick or slate instead of wood. (cited from: https://www.revolvy.com/main/index.php?s=Great%20Boston%20Fire%20of%201760)

New York 1835

Cause: On the night of December 16, 1835 a city watchman patrolling in the neighborhood smelled smoke. Approaching the corner of Pearl Street and Exchange Place, the watchman realized the interior of a five-story warehouse was in flames. He sounded alarms, and various volunteer fire companies began to respond. The situation was perilous. The neighborhood of the fire was packed with hundreds of warehouses, and the flames quickly spread through the congested maze of narrow streets. (cited from: https://www.thoughtco.com/new-yorks-great-fire-of-1835-1773780)

View of the Great Fire in New York, December 16th – 17th, 1835 by Nicolino Calyo. [1d]

Firefighting: The temperature was 17 degrees below zero. The East River was frozen. It was impossible to get water to the blaze, as it froze in the hoses. Every cistern and well was frozen. The firemen desperately stomped on the frozen hoses to try to clear them, but it didn't do much good. The water backed up from the hoses and spewed out, freezing almost instantly on the street. Citizens pitched in to help. Desperate for water to extinguish the blaze, firefighters tried to get water from the frozen river, breaking through the ice to get at the water below. The fire was finally put out after firemen blew up buildings around the inferno to create a firewall.

Damage: When the smoke finally cleared, more than 700 buildings were destroyed, including the last of the old historic Dutch buildings. Damages were estimated at between $20 million and $40 million. 23 of the city's 26 insurance companies were forced into bankruptcy.

Rebuild: Amazingly, in a year's time, every fire-ravaged block had been restored with buildings even more beautiful than before. The Fire Department, which had been generally disorganized, was slowly restructured. There were changes made to the way in which fires were fought. The greatest thing that resulted from the fire was that New York's antiquated water system was replaced with the biggest and most modern water system in the world – the Croton Water system. Millions of gallons of water would travel through 41 miles of stone tunnels from upstate New York to the outskirts of the city. Water would never be in short supply again. (cited from: https://nypost.com/2007/11/16/the-great-fire-of-1835-3/)

Chicago 1871

The Chicago Fire, 1871. [1e]

Cause: The fire started on October 8, 1871 in a barn on the O'Leary property at 137 DeKoven Street, there is no evidence it was caused by the poor woman's cow kicking over a lantern. That story was made up by newspaper reporter who later admitted he did so because he thought it made for more "colorful" copy. Modern researchers hypothesize that it may have actually been started by a transient smoking in the barn and inadvertently setting the hay inside on fire. Most of the city's buildings and sidewalks were made of wood and roofs were tar and shingles so the fire spread quickly.

Firefighting: In 1871, the Chicago Fire Department had 185 firefighters with just 17 horse-drawn steam engines to protect the entire city. The initial response by the fire department was quick, but due to an error by the watchman, the firefighters were sent to the wrong place, allowing the fire to grow unchecked. An alarm sent from the area near the fire also failed to register at the courthouse where the fire watchmen were in addition, firefighters were tired from having fought numerous small fires and one large fire in the week before. These factors combined to turn a small barn fire into a conflagration. Despite the fire spreading and growing rapidly, the city's firefighters continued to battle the blaze. A short time after the fire jumped the river, a burning piece of timber lodged on the roof of the city's waterworks. Within minutes, the interior of the building was engulfed in flames and the building was destroyed. With it, the city's water mains went dry and the city was helpless. The fire burned unchecked from building to building, block to block. The slums became kindling for the downtown blaze, where even the supposedly fireproof stone and brick buildings exploded in flames as the destruction swept northward. Only rainfall, the lake, and stretches of unbuilt lots on the North Side finally halted the wave of destruction on the morning of October 10. (cited from: https://en.wikipedia.org/wiki/Great_Chicago_Fire)

Damage: The fire devasted 3.3 square miles. 17,000 structures burned and 90,000 people were left homeless. Fortunately, it spread slowly enough that fewer than 300 died in the flames.

Rebuild: Despite the fire's devastation, much of Chicago's physical infrastructure, including its transportation systems, remained intact. Reconstruction efforts began quickly and spurred great economic development and population growth, as architects laid the foundation for a modern city featuring the world's first skyscrapers. At the time of the fire, Chicago's population was approximately 324,000; within nine years, there were some 500,000 Chicagoans. By 1890, the city was a major economic and transportation hub with an estimated population of more than 1,000,000 people and in 1893 Chicago hosted the World's Columbian Exposition, a tourist attraction visited by some 27.5 million people. (cited from: https://www.history.com/topics/great-chicago-fire)

Boston 1872

Cause: The fire started in the basement of a warehouse at 83-85 Summer Street, at the corner of Kingston Street, in the downtown area.

Federal Street Post Office in the wake of the Great Boston Fire of 1872. [1f]

Firefighting: The first alarm was received at 7:24 PM from Box 52 located at Summer and Lincoln Streets. The fire had nearly total possession of the building of origin upon the arrival of the first fire engine, Engine Co. 7 from their quarters at 7 East Street, near South Station. Hose Company 2, from Hudson Street, is credited with getting the first water on the fire. Additional alarms were struck at 7:29, 7:34, 7:45 and 8:00 PM. Further alarms were struck for Box 48 and Box 123. Urgent calls for help were sent by telegraph, but help was delayed due to many telegraph offices having closed for the evening. Firefighting units from Maine to Connecticut, arrived to help, but efforts to fight the fire were plagued by difficulties. There was not enough water on hand to get the fire under control; the hydrant system did not work well because much of the equipment was not standardized; and even when firefighters got their hands on an adequate supply of water, the height of the buildings and the narrowness of the streets made it difficult to direct the water at the blaze from the optimum angle. An equine epizootic epidemic had struck cities nationwide. In Buffalo 300 horses were dead in 24 hours. In Boston, of the city's fire department horses, 4 were dead and 24 unfit for duty so it was difficult to get the fire engines to the correct locations at the right times. In addition, some of the efforts were counter-productive; explosions were used to attempt fire breaks, but this high-risk strategy was not executed with enough precision and served only to further spread the fire. The fire was finally stopped at the doors of Fanueil Hall the following morning, but it had already destroyed much of the downtown area. (cited from: https://bostonfirehistory.org/fires/great-boston-fire-of-1872/ and https://www.history.com/this-day-in-history/fire-rips-through-boston)

Damage: The fire destroyed 776 buildings across 65 acres of land, with the assessed value of the properties at nearly $13.5 million and personal property loss of $60 million dollars.

Rebuild: Boston Fire Chief John Stanhope Damrell all but predicted the impending disaster after seeing the aftermath of the devastating 1871 Chicago Fire. Damrell had been pleading with the city since 1866 to install new hydrants, a steam engine, and larger pipes, but officials rejected his proposals. Boston learned from the disaster and quickly rebuilt a more spacious commercial district according to a new building code. In addition, the city approved increased funding to expand the fire department. The burnt district was quickly rebuilt. City planning during the post-fire reconstruction caused several streets in downtown Boston to be widened. Most of the rubble and ruins of the buildings destroyed by the fire was dumped in the harbor to fill in Atlantic Avenue. (cited from: https://www.boston.com/news/history/2017/11/09/when-an-1872-fire-ravaged-downtown-boston)

San Francisco 1906

Cause: On April 18, 1906 San Francisco experienced an 8.3 magnitude earthquake at 5:12 am. It was centered along the San Andreas Fault. Collapsed buildings and broken chimneys led to several large fires that soon coalesced into a city-wide holocaust.

Firefighting: The greatest obstacle to firefighting occurred when many of San Francisco's water and gas mains were ruptured. Leaking gas was the catalyst for fires that quickly spread. The entire alarm system went out at the first shock. As a result, not one alarm was ever sounded. The Fire Chief was killed in the initial quake making leadership a challenge. The main reservoirs for

Fire in San Francisco following the great earthquake of 1906. View if from Gold Gate Park, Marin County, California. (USGS) [1g]

the city were 20 miles away; 6 miles of the distance was disclosed to be along the quake's "fault line" and was destroyed. Other pipe lines turned out to be in filled ground and were broken. Water had to be sucked from the cisterns that were soon dry, even from the large main sewers. It was almost impossible to get feed or water for the horses, and sometimes even fresh water for the boiler. Near the waterfront fresh water was taken off ships for the engines. That's how scarce water was. On April 21, the fire simply stopped in the center of a block filled with wooden frame houses, ending three days of destruction. It was due to the fact that the San Francisco Fire Department was modern for its time that the Great Fire was not far more disastrous. (cited from: https://www.nps.gov/prsf/learn/historyculture/1906-earthquake-fire-fighting.htm andhttp://guardiansofthecity.org/sffd/fires/great_fires/1906/april_18_1906.html

Damage: Property loss was $350,000,000. The area burned was 4.7 miles square miles, which included all of the downtown territory. After the earthquake and fire 250,000 people were left homeless. They packed up what they had and left the city.

Rebuild: The old Victorian downtown was gone. The push was to build steel-framed, Class A buildings. San Francisco was a classic western boomtown before the quake and fire and had grown in a haphazard manner since the Gold Rush of 1849. Working from a nearly clean slate, the city was rebuilt with a more logical and elegant structure. The destruction of the urban center in San Francisco also encouraged the growth of new towns around the bay, making room for a new population boom arriving from the U.S. and abroad.

PART II - THE DEVELOPMENT OF INSURANCE AND FIRE DEPARTMENTS

The First System of Fire Insurance and Fire Departments

Considering the substantial losses caused by fires, it's understandable that systems of insurance would develop. Marcus Licinius Crassus lived in Ancient Rome (115–53 BC). He was one of the 10 most wealthy historical figures of all time. One of the ways he accumulated his wealth was by organizing one of the first fire brigades in history. When an area of Rome caught fire, Crassus' firemen would arrive, not do anything, and would negotiate a price to pay for all the property threatened by the fire. The price would go down by the minute as the fire continued and consumed the buildings and property. Only when property owners agreed to sell at 'fire sale' prices would the 500-man brigade pull down burning structures and put out the fire. Through the use of his fire brigade Crassus became one of the largest property owners in Rome. (cited from: http://dagblog.com/reader-blogs/firefighting-and-capitalism-marcus-licinius-crassus-obion-county-tennessee-7092)

Lead fire insurance marks, 2 of 3 insurance companies founded after the Great Fire of London in 1666. The one on the right displays the policy number 77903. This policy was issued to John Bezeley of St. Anne's, Middlesex who was a sugar refiner. The fire mark was on one of his tenements numbers 21, 2, 23 south of Rose Lane in Lime Street. He took out the policy originally on Jan. 23, 1758 and then renewed it with more buildings in 1765.

The earliest formal establishment of fire insurance came in 1681 following the Great Fire of 1666 in London. Dr. Nicholas Bardon, a doctor, economist and wealthy investor, realized that much of his wealth was in property. Together with 11 associates he established The Insurance Office for Houses at the back of the Royal Exchange and insured brick and frame homes. Other insurance schemes were established in the wake of the Great Fire. They were of 3 kinds: mutual insurance companies owned by the insured, private share-holder insurance companies and chartered insurance companies. To share the risks they took on, they resorted to reinsurance with others who took on the responsibility of underwriting their risks.

Lloyd's Subscription Room - 1809 [1h]

Edward Lloyd's tavern became the center of such underwriting activity. To protect their interest in the houses they insured, the fire insurance companies organized their own fire-fighting brigades. They issued to each householder they insured a "fire insurance mark" to be posted on the front of the home. The insurers' fire brigade would fight the fire in the house with their mark but let those without the mark burn. The mark was also meant to prevent fraudulent insurance claims for houses that burned down if they did not have the insurable company's mark posted. (cited from: "Where Have All the Horses Gone", p92)

The Early Development of Insurance and Firefighting in America

While the Ancient Roman fire "insurance" system was more beneficial for Crassus than the property owner and the early English fire insurance companies organized firefighting brigades to put out fires only at places they insured, the American experience was quite different.

New Amsterdam (now New York City) established the colonies first marshal system in 1647. Fire wardens inspected houses and chimneys and issued fines for potential hazards. An 8-man team called a "rattle watch" patrolled the streets at night. When a fire was detected, they shook wooden rattles to alert townspeople.

Boston's city fathers took the first steps in fire prevention when Governor John Winthrop outlawed wooden chimneys and thatched roofs in 1631. 40 years later, Boston suffered a series of arson fires and finally a conflagration in 1676. The small "engine" built by local ironmaker Joseph Jynks, probably a syringe-type pump, had little effect on the swelling wall of flames. Shortly after the fire, Bostonians sent for the "state of the art fire engine" then being made in England. The three-foot-long, 18-inch-wide wooden box arrived with carrying handles and a direct-force pump that fed a small hose. The tub-like section of the engine was kept filled with water by a bucket brigade. The need to coordinate these efforts brought about the establishment of the first engine company in colonial America. Twelve men and a captain were "hired" by the General Court to care for and manage the engine and to be paid for their work. On January 27, 1678, this company went into service. Its captain (foreman), Thomas Atkins, was actually the first firefighting officer in the country. (cited from: http://lishfd.org/History/firefighting_in_colonial_america.htm)

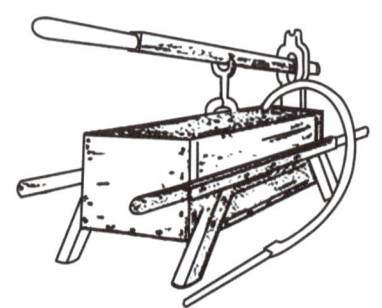

"State of the art Fire Engine" made in England.

The American Volunteer Fire Companies operated before the first fire insurance company was organized and acted independently. In 1736 Benjamin Franklin founded the Union Fire Company, America's first volunteer fire company. Later Franklin proposed organizing an insurance company to the members of the, by then, 8 volunteer fire companies. The new insurance company, "The Philadelphia Contributionship for the Insurance of Houses from Loss by Fire" formed in 1752. As was the practice of English insurers to identify insured property with a fire mark, the Contributionship adopted this practice. The fire mark selected was the symbol of four lead clasped hands mounted on a wood board. The clasped hands symbolized mutual support. These fire marks can still be seen on some buildings in Philadelphia.

Early 20th Century Philadelphia Contribution Fire Mark No. 906

Many famous Americans were volunteer firemen. George Washington joined the Alexandria Fire Department as a volunteer firefighter. In 1775 Washington purchased the town's very first fire engine. The image on the right depicts a young Washington pulling a fire pumper. (cited from: http://educationaltour.fasnyfiremuseum.com/1700-george-washington.html). Other famous early American volunteer firefighters include: Alexander Hamilton, John Hancock, Sam Adams and Paul Revere. In 1818 the first known female firefighter, Molly Williams, a black slave, rose to prominence in New York when she took her place with the men on the drag ropes and pulled the pumper to the fire through the deep snow.

A young George Washington pulling a wooden fire pumper. Later, as President, Washington often took the time to visit local fire companies; inquiring about developments in apparatus and talking with the firemen. [2]

Alexander Hamilton [3]   **John Hancock** [4]   **Sam Adams** [5]   **Paul Revere** [6]

The insurance company was an outgrowth of the firefighting companies, Article 15 of the Deed of Settlement stipulated that the company directors were to attend all "alarms of fire" to determine how best to serve the company and the public. Even though the early Philadelphia insurers from 1752 to about 1800 issued fire marks, unlike the English, they did not organize their own fire companies or acquire their own fire engines. The American volunteers fought all fires whether or not the property was insured, regardless of which company insured it, let alone have a fire mark. Fire marks were never required to designate a house as insured so that the firemen would fight the fire or that a reward would be forthcoming if they did. The fire mark indicated that the property was insured, but mostly, the mark served to advertise the company.

There is no evidence that volunteer fire groups in America did not put out the fires of houses without fire marks. The American volunteer fire service was founded on the principles of public service. It's unlikely the 18th century Philadelphia volunteer fire companies with such mottos as "Assist the needy, protect the weak" (Hibernia No.1), "Judge us by our actions" (Humane No. 13), and "To assist the citizens" (Philadelphia No. 18) would not fight fires on properties without a fire mark. Volunteer fire companies were prominent social organizations and membership was an honor. Having made their case for funding by proclaiming their work in the public interest, it seems unlikely they would disregard any fire that could cause a catastrophe.

Volunteer fire companies raced each other to be the first to "play" water on a fire; fire literature is replete with the intense rivalry and competition between engine companies. It was, and remains so today, a matter of great status to be the first company at a fire. In addition to municipalities paying rewards for the first to arrive at a fire, so did some insurance companies. First water rewards were offered by fire insurance companies in Boston, Cleveland, Hartford, Trenton, New Jersey, and Germantown Township, which was outside Philadelphia. (cited from: https://www.firemarkcircle.org/documents/goodstory.htm)

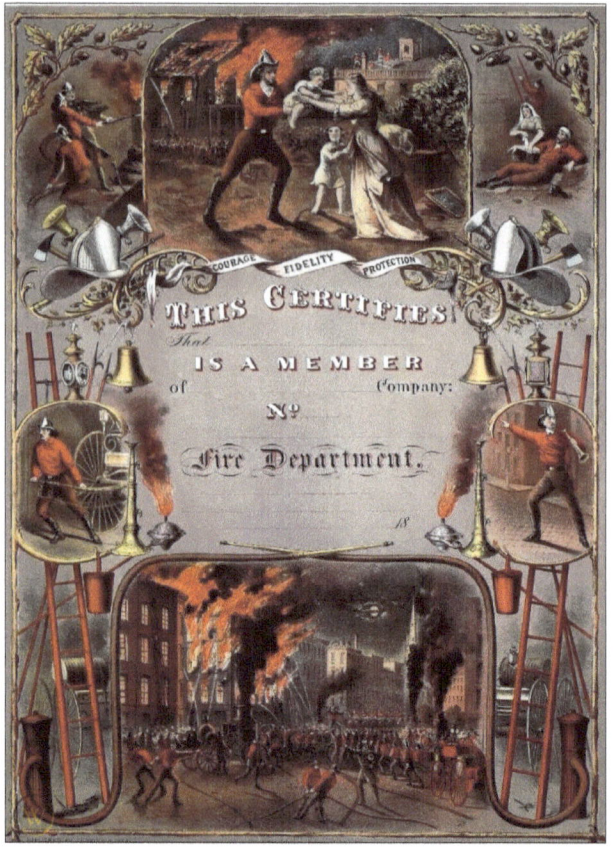

1800's Antique Fireman Fire Department FDNY, Certificate issued by Currier and Ives.

American firefighting began to evolve into a system of fraternal organizations, similar to the Masons or the Oddfellows. The volunteer firefighters of the early period were the most virtuous members of the early republic. They established themselves as manly heroes with mottoes in Latin, hearkening back to the republics of old. Currier and Ives issued membership certificates that depicted the hard work of the volunteers acting as heroes. These volunteer organizations served as fraternal organizations as well as fire companies. The reason men joined a fraternal society in this period was for things like death benefits for your family after you die, because there was no social safety net. It is certainly true that fire companies had rivalries that would turn physical. There were rivalries in cities like New York and Baltimore where fire companies would "go at it."

 (cited from: https://www.smithsonianmag.com/smithsonian-institution/early-19-century-firefighters-fought-fires-each-other-180960391/)

From the mid-18th to the mid-19th century, American cities tended to rely on volunteer groups or groups hired by insurance companies. Both methods turned out to provide exactly the wrong sort of motivation for serious firefighting. The volunteers were full of people that needed to prove how manly and tough they were, and the privately hired groups were offered bonuses. This meant that when different groups of firefighters from the same city met, they were as much in a mood to fight their rivals as they were to fight the fires, which they often did.

Eventually, the fact that firefighting was associated with violent brawls brought the attention of local gangs, which began associating themselves with firefighter units. In one particularly notorious example, a Philadelphia gang called "The Killers" joined the Moyamensing Hose Company in the 1840s. The violence quickly escalated to a point of absurdity: Firefighting companies were starting to set fires themselves. Naturally, firefighters also brought guns to their fights, and the exchanges could be quite lethal. A single 1856 confrontation in Lexington Market in Baltimore resulted in 7 deaths.

The consequences of lack of discipline were compounded by other elements that were attracted to the firehouses. It was a sign of professional prestige to get to the fire ahead of rival companies, and adversaries were prevented from getting to the scene too rapidly by "accidents." To maintain its right of way in a day of sheer force, a company might recruit plug-uglies to disable its opponents or their apparatus. Men who loved to brawl found that the fire department offered unbounded possibilities: opportunities to fight with policemen, shopkeepers who were too stingy about sharing their stocks, or, best of all, other firemen. Every alarm of fire became a grand, noisy adventure. The shouts of the firemen, the exuberant ringing of bells, and the sounds of human conflict worried respectable citizens. Equipment often was pulled along the sidewalks to the peril of pedestrians and merchandise. It was not unusual for a building to burn to the ground while two or more companies of firemen battled to see who should use the nearest hydrant or cistern. (cited from: http://www.americanheritage.com/content/how-steam-blew-rowdies-out-fire-departments)

A political cartoon depicting the Plug Uglies of Baltimore, MD, originally the Mount Vernon Hook and Ladder Volunteer Fire Company during the 1856 riots. [7]

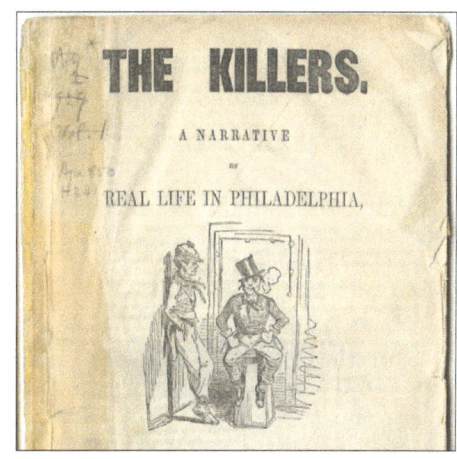

The cover page of George Lippard's The Killers likely shows two members representing the real south Philadelphia gang known as the Killers. The Irish gang that ruled the Moyamensing neighborhood in the 1840s was also known for its business in the fire hose industry. In this lithograph, one figure sits upon the nineteenth-century version of a fire hydrant, suggesting their allegiance to the organization.

The process by which all this came to an end started in Cincinnati, Ohio. They were the first city in America to have a regular, civil fire department. It was the precedent that turned firefighters from a literal public menace into national heroes. (cited from: http://knowledgenuts.com/2014/05/02/when-firefighters-were-actually-violent-gang-members/)

In 1850 alone, there were at least 6 major fights in Cincinnati in which two people were shot and dozens more injured and there were two arsons including the burning of Engine 02's firehouse. In 1853 Cincinnati inventors Alexander Latta and Abel Shawk create the "Uncle Joe Ross," the first practical steam fire engine. Given the concerns about discipline in the volunteer system, leading citizens in town recognized the potential of this invention and created the first full-time, paid professional fire department. An innovative model using professional firefighters and horse-drawn steam fire engines was created after a study of other approaches to fire protection around the county. This model set the standard for fire protection throughout the world for the next 60 years until the introduction of gasoline powered apparatus. (cited from: https://www.cincyfiremuseum.org/explore-the-museum/history/)

"OLD JOE ROSS" World's first practical steam fire engine. Built in Cincinnati 1852-53. Named after the city councilman who introduced legislation to buy the pumper for the city. [8]

Volunteer Fire Department in their parade-best. [9]

On festive occasions firemen dressed in their most colorful uniforms trying to outdo each other. Lavish helmets and uniforms, fancy fire axes, decorative parade torches, painted stovepipe-shaped "fire hats", fancy painted fire buckets and engraved silver speaking trumpets were commissioned for these parades. If they had a hand pumper, it too was decorated often by celebrated artists. (cited from: http://www.haverhillfirefightingmuseum.org/history-of-firefighting.php)

PART III – THE EVOLUTION OF FIREFIGHTING EQUIPMENT

Equipment and Methods for Fighting Fires

Water Pump: Heron/Hero (10 AD – 70 AD) a Greek mathematician and engineer improved the efficiency of the hand water pump, which was originally invented by the Greek engineer Ctesibius circa 200 BC. The Romans even used Hero's pump and a mechanical fire hose, to put out fires. Ctesibius's/Hero's pump, the sipho, described in ancient texts by Pliny and Vitruvius, was found in perfect condition after 2,000 years underground. It was used by Roman Vigiles, or firefighters, to put out fires, from a cistern and filled by hand bucket brigades. (cited from: http://www.foresightguide.com/50CE-a-steam-engine-in-ancient-rome/)

Cohort VII Vigiles. Each cohort, comprised a hundred men, had to ensure service in the territory of two regions and had a barracks in one of them and a guardhouse in the other. [12]

Roman Pump, Paris: Hierosme Drou̇ärt, 1624. [13]

The Ctesibius pump in the Museo Arqueológico Nacional. [10]

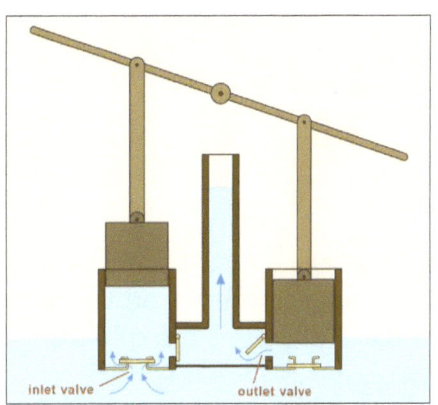

How the pump invented by Ctesibius works. Drawing by Tamás Lajtos. [11]

- 1204 – Sack of Constantinople (1204). Constantinople was burned three times during the Fourth Crusade. [174]
- 1212 – the Great Fire of Suthwark London 1212. The second of the two Great Medieval Fires of London. As many as 3,000 people died on the London Bridge while trying to flee the city.
- 1251 – Second Fire of Lübeck, Germany, triggers the use of stone as a fire-safe building material.
- 1253 – Great Fire of Utrecht, the Netherlands, lasted for 9 days and destroyed much of the city.
- 1276 – Third Fire of Lübeck, Germany, results in a comprehensive fire safety system. This was the last major fire in the city before bombing of WW II.
- 1327 – Fire of Munich, Germany, destroys one-third of the city, 30 deaths.
- 1405 – Fire of Bern, Switzerland, destroys 600 houses, over 100 deaths.
- 1421 – First Great Fire of Amsterdam, the Netherlands.
- 1438 – Great Fire of Gouda, the Netherlands, almost destroys the entire city.

Leather Buckets: In colonial times leather buckets, made by local cobblers, were the only means to transport water to the fire sites. The buckets held about 3 gallons of water. They were passed from hand to hand by lines of sturdy, male volunteers. When emptied they were returned by another line of boys and women, to be refilled. The buckets were painted and gilded with bright colors and patriotic symbols. They identified the Fire Company names and the date they were made. The most interesting have lavish illustrations. For almost a century these were the only way of putting water on the flames. (cited from: http://antiqueshoppefl.com/articles/april06/fire%20fighters.htm)

1793 Fire Bucket Leather [14]

Hand Pumpers: Bucket brigades were no match for conflagrations! A mechanical means of spraying water on fires was needed. One of the first people to make it practical was Richard Newsham of London. When fires broke out, men dragged the engines to the site and formed a bucket brigade to fill their reservoirs. Then the pumps were manned and water began to shoot out of a gooseneck nozzle emerging from the top. Philadelphia became the first colonial city to acquire one of Newsham's machines, ordering a pair in 1730. New York City did the same the following year, and Salem, Massachusetts, ordered one in 1749. So effective were Newsham's engines that some were used for more than a century.

Fire Extinguishers: Early fire extinguishers were primitive, ineffective, and sometimes dangerous. Glass bulb "water grenades" [c.1910] were designed to be thrown at a blaze, breaking the glass and releasing fire

1744-65 Artist/Maker Richard Newsham [15]

Left: Early fire extinguishers - Tube and Bulb versions [16]

dousing "vaporizing liquid." The bulbs contained carbon tetrachloride, a hazardous chemical outlawed by the state in 1962. Tube fire extinguishers hung on walls, ready to be grabbed in emergencies. When pulled from their wall hooks, the tubes opened and dispensed fire suffocating powder, "guaranteed never to cake harden." (cited: https://sandiegohistory.org/journal/1989/april/eating/)

Hoses: Leather fire hoses, invented in 17th-century Holland, leaked and needed too much care to be very useful. In 1808, a Philadelphia company devised a method of closing the seams with copper rivets; leather hoses quickly made buckets obsolete. However, they still needed constant maintenance with grease and oil to keep them from drying and cracking. With the arrival of canvas and rubber hoses in the 1820s, firefighters thankfully said goodbye to leather hoses forever.

Leather Hose [17]

Hose Carts: were used to transport the lengths of fire hoses. These carts were typically two wheel affairs, with each wheel being a good five feet in diameter. Larger four-wheeled carts were also used, but were more expensive and required more space and men to haul it.

The fireman's hose cart races were one of the first larger public athletic events in many areas. The local firemen would show their athletic skills before crowds of 1,000 people or more, racing to be the pride of the County. With family and loved ones watching with great admiration, the winners would receive a coveted silver trophy cup. (cited. https://www.marinfirehistory.org/hose-cart-racing.html)

A two-wheeled hose cart, with nozzles, tool storage box, lanterns, and rope reels for the men to unroll and help pull the cart. The black rotating bar behind the hose reel was used to help the hose lay out without getting caught up underneath. [18]

The Saugatuck Fire Department in Michigan. Photo courtesy Saugatuck-Douglas Historical Society. [20]

The Larkspur VFD Team practicing with their chemical fire cart - chemical tanks replaced the fire hose to create water pressure, and usually ran in tandem with hose carts. [19]

Fire Alarms: The first fire alarm was somebody seeing smoke and yelling. By the mid-19th century New York City had a series of 8 watchtowers manned by sentries looking for signs of flame. In 1852 a Boston doctor named William Channing invented an alarm system that could send a telegraph signal from a street box to an alarm office. Entrepreneur John Gamewell purchased the patent for the technology in 1859, and, three decades later, he dominated the market with alarms in 500 cities nationwide. Soon every big city had telegraph alarm boxes, which lasted until the 1970s, when more efficient telephone systems were developed.

Fireboats: Ship and dock fires were once regular occurrences in every American port. In 1800 New York firefighters built the first fireboat; a hand-pumped engine attached to a barge. In 1867 New York hired a tugboat for putting out fires and outfitted it with hoses and other equipment. In 1873 the Boston Fire Department launched the William F. Flanders, the first fireboat specifically built for that purpose. New York City's largest fireboat, Fireboat Three Forty Three of Marine Company 1, is one of the most powerful pieces of fire apparatus ever built, capable of pumping 50,000 gallons of water every minute.

Gamewell & Co. purchased the rights and title to the electromagnetic fire alarm telegraph for cities up to 1871. [25]

1857 - William Channing and Moses Farmer received a patent for a fire alarm telegraph. [26]

"The New Yorker" 1891 - Engine Co. 57
The battle-scarred veteran was the first fireboat to have a permanent shore station at Pier I, N.R. [29]

Fire boats fighting five alarm Charlestown fire - 1930

Fireboat Three Forty Three of Marine Company 1
FDNY's largest fireboat [27]

"FIRE ENGINE No. 31"—THE NEW FIRE BOAT IN USE IN BOSTON HARBOR.

March 1, 1890 - Scientific American, A weekly journal of practical information, art, science, mechanics, chemistry, and manufactures. Vol. LXII. Est. 1845. New York, NY. 28

THE NEW BOSTON FIRE BOAT " ENGINE NO. 3!."

The city of Boston has recently built and put into service a fire boat, designed for use as a floating fire engine. As the vessel in question represents the most advanced type of fire boat, and in a number of points differs from any hitherto constructed, we illustrate it in this issue. The construction of boats of this kind has now been developed until they are no longer mere tug boats with special pumps. Everything in their design is intended to insure the production of a true floating fire engine, one that for days in succession, without a minute's intermission, can throw water upon burning buildings or shipping. Thus on the occasion of the burning of the great elevators of the New York Central Railroad in this city, in May, 1889, the New York Fire Department boat Havemeyer was kept at work for nineteen days and nights, her boiler being under forced draught for that period. This, of course, was a highly exceptional occurrence. There are but few structures in New York and its environs that would require such heroic treatment if burning. Yet it shows what a fire boat may be called on to perform.

The new Boston fire boat is named "Engine No. 31," and has no other title. The general dimensions are as follows : Length over all, 108 feet ; on water line, 97 feet ; beam, maximum, 24½ feet ; on water line, 23 feet : depth of hold, 8 feet 1 inch ; draught, 7 feet 4 inches. The hull is of wood, and is of extra strength to resist the exceptionally heavy strains to which the heavy machinery will subject it. The best quality of white oak is used for the principal members of the frame and for the plan king. Hackmatack and yellow pine are used for upper frames and other parts. Below the waterline the hull is sheathed with yellow metal.

The stem under the water curves upward very gradually from the keel, and from a point about two feet above the water line downward and aft for about twenty feet carries a yellow metal shoe, one-half inch thick. On the hurricane deck, or above the main deck house, is the pilot house and the officers' house and drying room. The cabins in the main deck house include officers' cabin and main cabin, galley, mess room, and general offices. Accommodations for a crew of fourteen wen and officers are provided in this house.

The steam is generated by Cowles' water tube boilers. There are two of these, each occupying an area of 11½ X 7⅓ feet, and in height rising 11½ feet. When filled with water and ready for use the two weigh 19 '74 tons. They have 3,200 square feet of heating surface, a little over 87 square feet of grate'surface, and are tested up to 300 pounds, giving a working allowance of 200 pounds. With natural draught they develop 400 horse power, which may, by steam jets in the chimney, be brought up to 900 horse power. This boiler is a sort of combination tube and shell ...

(Read full article in Image Sources)

Water Main: Until the early 19th century firefighters had to rely on wells, rivers, ponds, and reservoirs for water. If one of these wasn't nearby, the building burned to the ground. New York City's first water mains were hollowed-out logs. They leaked and clogged, but they were better than nothing. In 1808 one was fitted with the first fire plug; a sort of large cork. The first real fire hydrant came in 1817. Today firefighters in most high-rise areas use high-pressure mains as their source of water.

A wood-stave pipe. As early as the late 1800's they were building continuous wood-stave pipes in the 12 and 14 feet diameter size for literally miles of water transfers. Instead of all being the same length and built flush with each other, this construction method staggered the staves so that pipe building would just go on and on until you got to where you were going. [22]

Log water pipes being excavated in 1936; these were well over 200 years old when dug up. [23]

A hollowed log fire main with several fire plugs. Firefighters would have to dig a hole to reach the pipe, then drill through the wooden pipe to intentionally create a leak. The hole would fill with water so the fire engines could pump it out. This brings an all new meaning to the term "Shoveling hydrants"! After the incident the firefighters would seal the hole with a wooden plug, hence the term "fire plug". [21]

A wooden fire-plug (ancestor of the metal fire hydrant) is seen embedded in the sidewalk at the curb in front of the horse-drawn Ice Wagon. Napoleon House, New Orleans, Louisiana. Photo 1900 - 1906. [24]

Ladders: As buildings rose to 5, 7, and even 10 stories, firefighters had to figure out how to keep up. In 1882 the FDNY (Fire Department of New York) purchased French-made scaling ladders (Pompier Ladder); short ladders with hooks on one end that could be moved up floor by floor. The Pompier ladders were in use until 1996. Today aerial ladders can reach as high as 130 feet, and they ride on special ladder trucks. After the tragic consequences of the first skyscraper fires, however, fire departments realized that they needed a whole new array of tactics. After 146 people died in the Triangle Shirtwaist factory fire, in 1911, citizen outrage led to a wholesale revamping of New York City's fire code. Buildings had to strictly control the storage of flammable materials; fire doors had to open; fire escapes had to be firmly attached; and sprinkler systems were required in every factory. Other cities followed suit, usually after their own deadly fires, as people realized that the best way to stop fires is to keep them from starting.

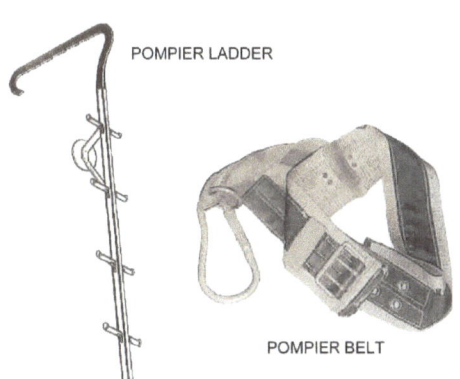

Pompier Ladder - French-made scaling ladders. The top of the ladder, with its iron catch, would be hooked over a window sill, and the firefighter would climb the narrow rungs to the window. [30]

Boston Firefighter's demonstrating the use of Pompier ladders in 1935. Although these ladders are rarely used today, all Boston Firefighter's must be proficient in their use. It is one of the last skills test that recruits must complete to graduate. [31]

As more height is needed, another pompier ladder would be passed up to the top firefighter and he would raise it to the next window and repeat the process. [30]

- *1452 – Second Great Fire of Amsterdam, the Netherlands, destroys three-quarters of the city.*
- *1544 – Burning of Edinburgh - An English amphibious raid destroyed portions of the city and many surrounding villages.*
- *1547 – The 1547 Moscow fire sparked a rebellion.*
- *1571 – The 1571 Moscow fire occurred when the forces of the Crimean khan Devlet I Giray raided the city.* [175]

- *1608 – First settlement in Jamestown, New York burnt.*
- *1615 – Great Fire of Wymondham, Norfolk, England, two simultaneous fires destroyed 300 properties.*
- *1624 – Oslo, Norway, destroyed by fire.*

The Life of a Fireman - The Night Alarm - 1854
Throughout his prints of fire fighting, Louis Maurer emphasized accuracy. Here, a group of firemen from Excelsior Company No. 2, of 21 Henry Street, New York City, are shown pulling a pumper-wagon from the firehouse in response to a night alarm. The clock inside the firehouse reads 1:22. At the left, Nathaniel Currier, a volunteer fire fighter with the company, runs to join his colleagues, James Merritt Ives and George B. Ives. [32]

Steam Pumpers: Many volunteer fire companies fought tooth and nail against the purchase of the first steam-powered fire engines. At demonstrations, the men proved they could pump harder and shoot water higher than the early smoke-belching machines. But for government officials, the clincher was that the steam-powered engines never got tired. Starting in Cincinnati in the 1850s, every major city switched over to steam. By the turn of the century the most powerful of these could generate more pressure than the average modern-day fire engine. The steam engines were heavy. The tongue on the steam pumpers stuck out in front six feet. Many streets were not paved in those days and it took approximately 20 men to pull the steam engines with 7 or 8 more men pulling the hose cart. 4 men held the tongue on the steam pumper while others pulled ropes. The critical job of those pulling were the men on the tongue. The head man at the right of the tongue did the guiding around the corners and through the ruts. It was also the men on the tongue's job to see that the wagon did not overtake the runners. It was not unheard of for a man to be run over if he fell. These steam pumpers were much too heavy for men to pull them to the fires in time to be useful. (cited from: https://www.americanheritage.com/content/tools)

PART IV – THE FIRE HORSE SAVES THE DAY

The Need for Horses

Before fire departments employed fire horses, some fire departments occasionally used a horse for various jobs. In 1816 Engine 29 of the old New York City volunteers enjoyed the strength of "Skinny", a horse owned by one of the members, to aid in pulling the engine if there was a man shortage or danger of the machine becoming mired, but he was not employed regularly.

When fire broke out in Bayard Street, New York, in May, 1828, and spread to the Bowery, 3 horses brought the Yorkville engine down to help the New Yorkers. This may have been the original of the 3-horse hitches. Records of the New York Mutual Hook & Ladder Company No. 1 show that the organization bought a horse in 1832 for $88; one of the reasons may have been due to a shortage of firefighters caused by a yellow fever epidemic. The other stations were unsympathetic. One evening the anti-equine element crept into the stable, shaved the horse's mane and tail and painted a white stripe down the horse's back, embarrassing the company. To add insult to injury, the Oceanus volunteers beat the horse-drawn Mutuals to a fire. The horse was sold the next year. During the early days of New York's volunteers, horses added to the pageantry of parades. When celebrating the opening of the Erie Canal, Nov. 4, 1825, many of the companies exhibited their beautifully painted and burnished engines on cars drawn by horses. The floats were covered with draperies and drawn usually by four horses.

Europe employed horses long before America. At first there was resistance to the use of horses in America. All the apparatus in use had been especially designed and constructed to be drawn by hand. The substitution of horse power for man power in the department would have required so few men that the social and political features of the fire department would have been weakened. There would also have been a heavy expense involved as new apparatus would have to be purchased and appropriations made for the construction of stables, as well as to defray the cost of remodeling the houses, and the cost of feed and harnesses and of course, horses.

Some fire departments DID put the cart before the horse because they had no horses! In 1900 the Bellevue, Ky fire department purchased its first horse drawn fire equipment - a hose and ladder wagon for the volunteer firemen, but the city lacked money for a horse to pull the wagon. As firefighters have done throughout history, Bellevue's bravest improvised. When an alarm sounded, the firefighters would commandeer the first horse in sight, unhitch the animal from the wagon he was pulling and harness him to the fire wagon. Some horse owners were said to give battle during this practice in fear of harm to the animal. More often, the horse would object by rearing, kicking and snorting.
(cited from: https://fdbd.org/about-fdbd/history/history-of-the-bellevue-fire-department/)

Bellevue, Ky Fire Department - 1900 [33]

Not until paid departments were created did the horse have an established part in fire protection. The paid fire department came a few years before the Civil War. Cincinnati, Boston, St. Louis and Baltimore were pioneers in this innovation. With the introduction of the paid force, the horse was employed, being accepted as necessary for efficiency, both in speed of response and in reducing the number of men needed to manually pull the engines and apparatus. The expansion of cites, with more distance to cover, and the size and weight of the steam engines exhausted the men pulling them. At the close of the Civil War Baltimore mustered 34 horses in its department, Cincinnati 70 horses. New York was just changing from volunteers to paid so they had no horses. John Cornwall introduced the horse to New York's fire service. As captain, and later as superintendent of the fire patrol maintained by the underwriters, Cornwall urged the use of horses in the late 1850's. Unable to convince his superiors of the advantage his plan would give, he supplied teams for 2 months at his own expense. 3 wagons were used and the efficiency of the horse-drawn equipment, always first at a fire, was apparent. In 1865, New York organized its paid battalion, horses thereupon replacing men as power. The change was welcomed by the majority of citizens. Commenting on this phase of the new department, Augustine E. Costello, in his history of the metropolitan firemen, wrote, "The horses did not yell and urge each other to exertion on the way to a fire, but attended strictly to business and left the camp followers who were not the fleetest of foot in the lurch, so that the pranks and depredations of the sidewalk committees were done away with. The horses, too, had no fancy for hurrying to rush past a rival company, or halt and fight out rancorous sentiment, partly jealousy, partly rivalry, while the fire which had started was getting ahead." (cited from: http://www.mi-harness.net/publct/tpr/firehorse.html and http://guardiansofthecity.org/sffd/firehorses/chapter1.html)

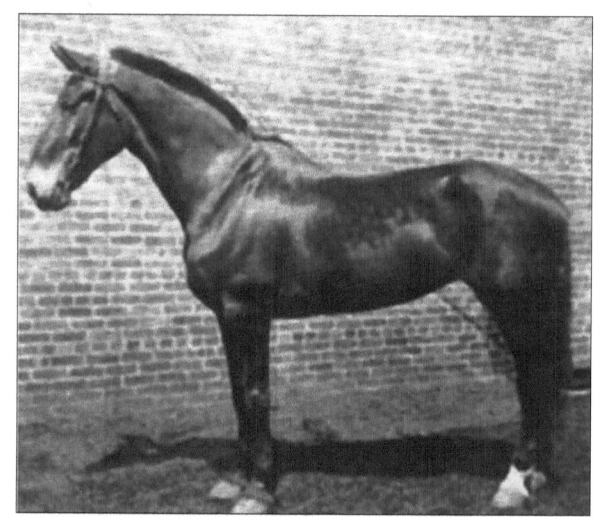

"Old Kit" first fire horse of the Gloversville, New York department. [34]

To this day many fire departments fondly remember the first horse purchased by the fire department. The first horse purchased for the Gloversville, New York department was "Old Kit" and soon after, 2 more horses were purchased. It has been said Old Kit could take a corner going 60 miles an hour. (cited from: http://www.cityofgloversville.com/old-kit/)

Over time the feeling that, "A firehouse ain't no place for no stinkin' horse!" changed. At first horses were stabled near the stations. When the alarm sounded, it took valuable time to unlock the barn, fetch the steeds and harness them to the engine. Before long, the horses lived at the station and the reluctance to accept them was replaced by a deep affection for the noble animals. (cited from: http://firehistory.weebly.com/a-history-of-horses-in-the-fire-service.html)

Horse Drawn Vehicles

Steam engine/pumper: The most efficient firefighting appliance was the horse-drawn steam pumper. This comprised a vertical water tube boiler providing steam for a pumping engine to force water through the hoses onto a fire. All this machinery was mounted on a horse-drawn sprung carriage with four steel-rimmed wooden wheels. The steam fire engine was invented in 1829 by John Braithwaite, partner in the engineering firm of Brathwaite and Ericsson of London. The typical "steamer" included a boiler and two direct-acting steam pumps mounted on wheels and drawn by horses. The firebox was water-jacketed and was provided with a forced draught by a mechanical bellows, while the exhaust gas issued from a funnel behind the driver's seat. Some engines could throw as much as 900 gallons of water per minute the length of a football field. During the Great San Francisco fire, there were so many steam engines working that the pressure pulled the wooden water mains right out of the ground. They sent 13 of their 28 pumpers down to the ocean for the water supply and the engines continued pumping for 8 days. They were unaware what the salt water would do to the inside of a boiler and all 13 were ruined.

Union Engine No. 3 - York, PA., fire department, 1910-1920. [35]

The steam pumper made it possible to supply continuous water to the scene of the fire. When horses started pulling equipment and apparatus it lessened the need for manpower. Although the horses transported the apparatus to the fire, the firefighters still arrived by foot.

Horse-drawn Engine, Newton, MA 1880. [38]

1894 Silsby Fourth Size Horse-Drawn Steam Pumper. [37]

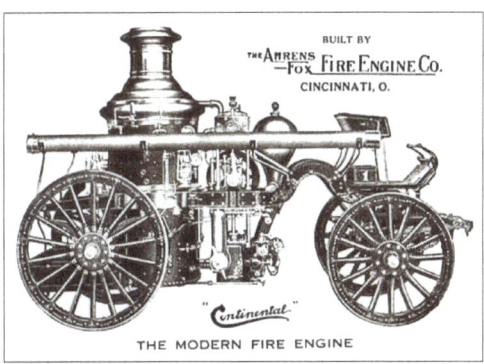

Ahrens-Fox Fire Engine Company, Cincinnati, Ohio 1910-1977. [36]

Hose Wagon: For more than 200 years, hose – that highly portable, flexible means of getting water onto the fire – has been the most important basic tool in the firefighter's arsenal of weapons. Early, riveted leather fire hose was heavy and bulky, from the onset requiring some kind of cart to get it to the fire

Ultimately, a cylindrical reel on which the hose could be wound, then quickly played out at the fire scene, proved the most efficient way to store and transport fire hose. From the mid to late 1800s, horse-drawn two wheeled or four wheeled hose reels typically accompanied the steam fire engine to fires.

Horse-drawn two wheeled hose reel [39]

By the late 19th century, in larger town and cities, the hose was more commonly carried in an open-top hose wagon, rather than on a reel. In the early years of the last century, many hose wagons were equipped with soda and acid chemical equipment. Typically drawn by two horses,

Horse-drawn four wheeled hose wagon once in the Gloria Austin Collection. [42]

Horse-drawn four wheeled hose reel [40]

Combination Hose and Chemical Wagon, #3 Battle Creek, Michigan. [41]

these dual-purpose rigs were known as Combination Hose Wagons. Some big-city hose wagons also had fixed turret nozzles attached to their sides. Today's modern plasticized fire hose, including large-diameter master stream supply lines, takes up far less space on the apparatus than the old cotton, rubber-lined hose once did. It's easier to handle, pack and dry, too, with quick-release Storz couplings.
(cited from: http://www.windsorfire.com/windsors-early-hose-wagons/)

Chemical Unit: The horse-drawn chemical wagon was developed to quickly fight the fire while the steam pumper was being prepared. The wagons carried tanks that were filled with bicarbonate of soda and activated by mixing with sulfuric acid. The resulting chemical reaction shot into the air through a small hose. (cited from: https://www.firedex.com/blog/2011/10/21/early-fire-apparatus-the-horse-drawn-era/) Large cities had separate Steam Companies and Chemical Companies.

- *1625 – First Great Stockholm Fire, Sweden, burned for three days and destroyed a fifth of the infrastructure.*
- *1652 – Glasgow, Scotland, a third of the city destroyed and over 1,000 families left homeless.*
- *1653 – Great Fire of Marlborough, England, destroyed the Guildhall, St Mary's Church, the County Armoury, and 224 dwellings.*
- *1656 – Fire of Aachen destroys 4,664 houses, kills 17.*
- *1657 – Great Fire of Meireki destroys two-thirds of the Japanese capital Edo (modern-day Tokyo).*
- *1663 – Great Fire of Nagasaki destroys the port of Nagasaki in Japan.*
- *1666 – Great Fire of London. Read Samuel Pepys diary entry on London fire, Sunday, Sept 2, 1666. Rumored to start in a bakers house. https://www.pepysdiary.com/diary/1666/09/02/. If you read on, you will learn there are many stories for how the fire was started. https://www.pepysdiary.com/encyclopedia/10872/ and https://www.pepysdiary.com/diary/1667/02/24/* [176]

1890 Holloway with two 50 gallon soda-acid chemical tanks. [43a]

Large cities had separate Steam Companies and Chemical Companies. In 1890 Chemical 1, of the Seattle Fire Department, moved to a temporary quarter with their equipment after the Great Seattle Fire of 1889. [44a]

Chemical Unit Truck #1 - Wenatchee, WA Fire Department, 1911. [44]

Horse-drawn Chemical Unit Truck once in the Gloria Austin Collection. 1908 engine that was used by the volunteers of Phoenix, Arizona from 1908 to 1914. The maker was the Anderson Coupling Company of Kansas City, Missouri. [45]

Horse-Drawn Chemical Engine #1, 1889 Champion with two 80-Gallon Soda-Acid Chemical Tanks. [43]

Horse-Drawn Water Tower #1
1904 Champion 65' Water Tower with 1100 GPM Monitor at Station 10 - 3rd Ave S & S Main St. Seattle, WA. [48]

Water Tower: The horse-drawn water tower was fed through inlets on the sides of the deck from several steam fire engines or from a pressurized hydrant. Water pressure was used to raise the tower to a vertical position. Then the water could be pumped up the 65-foot tower and put onto the fire. (cited from: http://www.firegold.com/2waterTower.html)

Water Tower and Ladder Wagon, 1925. [58]

Fire at coal yard, South Boston, MA, with water tower in action, 1911. Notice the two little boys sitting on the building across the street from the fire. [47]

On Dec. 28, 1925, a five-alarm fire struck the George J. Mueller Candy Company at 336 Pennsylvania Ave., Northwest, in Washington's Chinatown.

The Washington Post said:
"The much-maligned water tower, which has failed at so many big fires, was given credit for checking the fire. The tower was lofted to a position directly in front of the blaze.

"For an hour it hurled water into the building, the stream being pumped by four engines." [46]

Ladder Trucks: Firefighters were faced with a particular challenge - some of the most damaging fires experienced in American cities in the mid-19th century were in multi-story buildings. For many years inventors had tried to develop a hook and ladder truck that would effectively reach the upper levels of contemporary buildings, but initial attempts at aerial ladder trucks were often disastrous. Too heavy or too unstable, these horse-drawn trucks were either unable to reach fires in a timely manner or did not function well at the scene of a fire. In several cases, these early models cost the lives of firefighters who scaled their unsafe ladders. Then, in 1868, Daniel Hayes developed a truck with an aerial ladder that could extend as much as 85 feet in height.

The Hayes Aerial Ladder Truck - 65 foot Aerial Ladder Truck began service as a Volunteer Company in 1884 known as the Vigilance Hook & Ladder No. 1, located downtown at Aliso and Alameda. [50]

Horse-Drawn 1889 Preston 65' Aerial Ladder Truck #8. Aerial shortened to 55' in 1911. 1912 at Station 18 - Russell Ave NW & NW Market St. Seattle, WA. [51]

Horse-drawn ladder truck from a Seagrave factory photo. Close up of a curved hook and a flat hook on a ladder truck, 1890's. In Matt Lee's book, A Pictorial History of the Fire Engine – Volume I, he explains, "The curved hook is for pulling down buildings or portions of buildings in order to create a fire break. The flat hook, with a pulley in its base, was for hoisting items over a roof or wall." [49]

The ladder truck was set up so that the tillerman could sit underneath it and firefighters would raise, rotate and extend the aerial ladders using gears and pulleys they cranked by hand; 4 to 6 men could fully raise the telescopic ladder in less than 40 seconds. The aerial was mounted on a turntable, so the ladder could be swung around to the desired direction. Hayes had designed, and then built himself, the first practical and safe horse drawn aerial ladder truck. The truck was named after its inventor: the Hayes Extension Hook and Ladder Truck and Fire Escape.

Horse-Drawn 1906 American LaFrance 85' Tillered Aerial Ladder Truck #2, Seattle, WA. [52]

Demand increased as word of the practicality and reliability of Hayes' aerial ladder truck design spread across the United States. In 1884, Hayes sold his patent to the New York-based LaFrance Company (soon to become American LaFrance). A number of sizes were developed to meet the distinctive needs of various cities' fire departments;

American LaFrance Hayes Aerial Ladder, 1902. [54]

models ranged from a "first class" truck with an 85-foot extension ladder to the small "fourth class" truck featuring a 40 or 45-foot extension ladder. (cited from: https://www.lafra.org/lafd-history-hayes-aerial-ladder-truck/) Eventually running boards were installed on the sides of the ladder trucks, making it possible for the firefighters to ride to the scene of the fire. The name "running boards" came from the fact that they took the place of firefighters running to the fire. Imagine how this improved a firefighter's ability to fight the fire once he arrived, no longer exhausted from the run.

Ladder Truck at the George J. Mueller Candy Company in Chinatown, WA, 1925. [53]

Horse-Drawn Chief's Buggy - Between 1909 & 1913 at Station 4 - 4th Ave N & Thomas St. Seattle, WA. [55]

Horse-drawn Chief's Buggy once in the Gloria Austin Collection. [56]

Horseshoeing equipment - 1916 at Station 25, Harvard Ave & E Union St. Seattle, WA. [57]

Chief's Buggy: The Fire Chief arrived at the fire in his own vehicle. Most often these vehicles were "Runabouts" or "Concord Wagons". Runabouts and Concord Wagons are American open vehicles with four large wheels and are not encumbered with fenders, heavy tops or optional accessories that would add weight. They are light in order to be easily pulled at speed over long distances by a single horse. A century ago, men who served their communities as police officers and fire fighters were revered by their neighbors and held in high esteem. It was a source of great pride in a community to parade the local fire equipment for all to see. The ceremonial phaeton made in 1909 by Studebaker was reserved for the Fire Chief's personal use on such occasions and would have been put to the department's most reliable horse. A bell on the floor of the carriage was pumped by the occupant to alert onlookers of their arrival. Both the sound of the bell and the excitement of the parade demanded a horse's best behavior. Painted white to accentuate the beautiful lamps. The carriage, horse and harness would represent the department's finest efforts. The lamp on the rear of the vehicle is removable and can be carried in hand to illuminate the way.

Horseshoeing Wagon: The horse's shoes were checked on a daily basis; runs on paved, trolley tracks and brick and cobblestone streets were hard on the shoes. Often calks and corks needed to be added to ensure that the horses would not slip. The farrier traveled from station to station and sometimes went out on runs to make repairs or replace shoes on the spot.

Supply Wagon - 1900 [58]   **Debris Wagon - 1911** [59]   **Coal Wagon - 1916** [60]

Supply Wagon: Many fire departments also had a supply wagon to carry baskets of coal, grenades, extra hose, brooms, buckets, pikes, axes and other equipment that would be needed at the scene of the fire.

Insurance Patrol: In the early days of firefighting, insurance companies and fire departments worked together at a fire scene. Fire patrols were organized by insurance companies to cover a neighborhood and report any fires that occurred, inspect buildings for fire hazards, and work with the fire department to prevent loss of life and property. Patrol wagons were equipped with rubber blankets to protect property from water damage, fire extinguishers, and buckets to squelch small fires and would pump water from cellars and mop it up from roofs after the fire was extinguished.

Insurance Patrol [61]

Horse Ambulance: Many of the very first horse trailers were actually horse-drawn ambulances used by city fire departments. Horse injuries were common at city accidents and they needed a way to quickly transport wounded but savable horses back to the firehouse for veterinary care. (cited from: https://www.doubledtrailers.com/13-fascinating-facts-about-horse-trailer-history/)

Horse-drawn Ambulances used by City Fire Departments [62a]   **The ASPCA operates the first ambulance for injured horses, NYC - 1867** [62]

Harness and Other Equipment

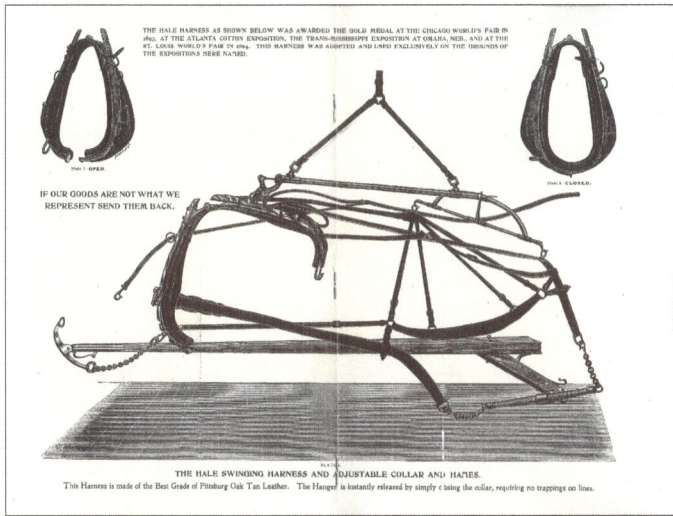

Ad fo the Hale Swinging Harness with Adjustable Collar and Hames [67]

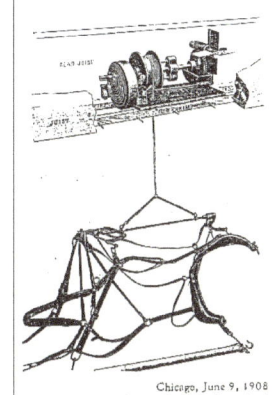

Ad for accessory to improve the operation of the Quick Hitch Harness.[68]

Interior, apparatus floor, quick hitch system suspended from ceiling, 1907. [64]

Quick Hitch Harness: Many fire chiefs and firemen invented various versions of a quick hitch harness; of these, George Hale and Charles Berry are the best known. The quick hitch harness was a model of simple perfection. Not an unnecessary strap or buckle was used. There was no crupper or belly band, a breeching which fell naturally over the flanks met the strain of a hold back, the collar formed the leverage for the pull. This collar locked automatically upon being pressed together, and snaps attached the reins to the bit rings. The entire harness, save the straight bitted bridle which the fire horse wore constantly, was attached to pole and whiffletrees and held high above the floor upon a swinging frame, operated by a pulley which permitted it to be lowered instantly, the frame swinging upward as soon as it was tripped by the harness dropping upon the animal's back. Two motions harnessed a horse-the thrust of the open collar together, another movement of both hands simultaneously snapping reins into the bit rings. The driver had leaped to his seat and seized the lines, and as his associates completed the hitching he urged his team forward while the crew scrambled aboard as the rig rolled from the house. (cited from: http://www.mi-harness.net/publct/tpr/firehorse.html)

Some unique features of the harness included:

The Quick Hitch Collar: which greatly reduced harnessing time. The hames were permanently attached; the collar opened with a latch at the bottom and had a hinge at the top over the withers. Reins and girths (if used) clipped on instead of buckled.

Reins and girths: (if used) clipped on instead of buckled. Bridles were often some kind of halter-bridle or had clip-on bits. Some fire departments' horses wore more normal bridles around the clock; they had to be taken off when the horses were fed grain, which could cause problems if there was an alarm during mealtime.

Bridles: did not have blinkers for safety reasons. Horses had to be able to see on their own in order to navigate through traffic at high speeds

If more than two horses were needed to pull a vehicle, (the usual hitch was three horses abreast to keep the hitch compact for city driving) the reins buckled together so that the driver only had one right and left rein to hold. (cited from: http://atomicstables.blogspot.com/2013/02/fire-department-harness-part-3-harness.html)

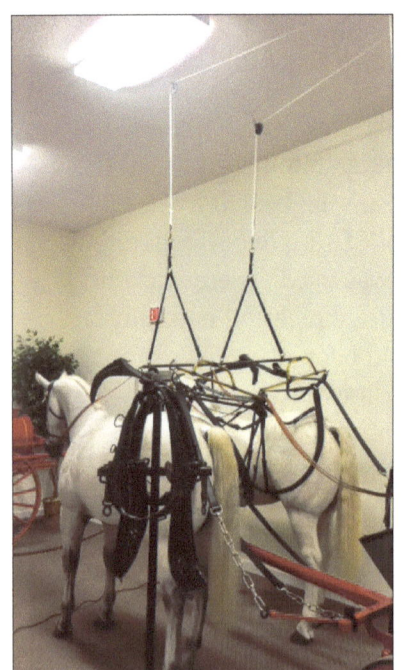
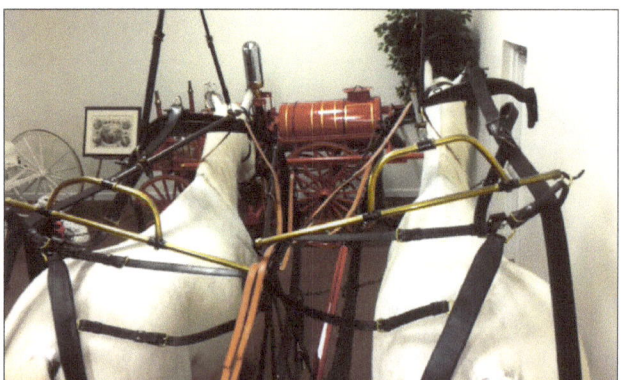
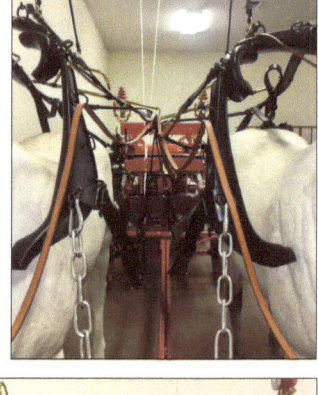
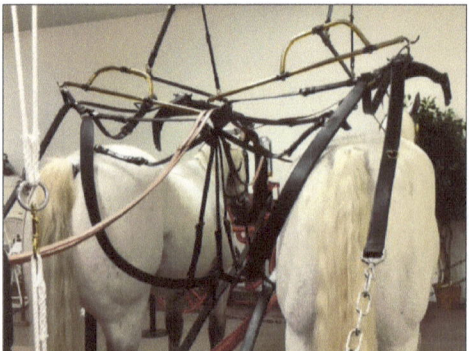
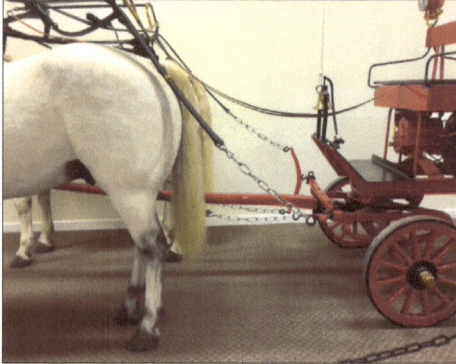

Quick Hitch Collar once on display in the Gloria Austin Collection. [66]

 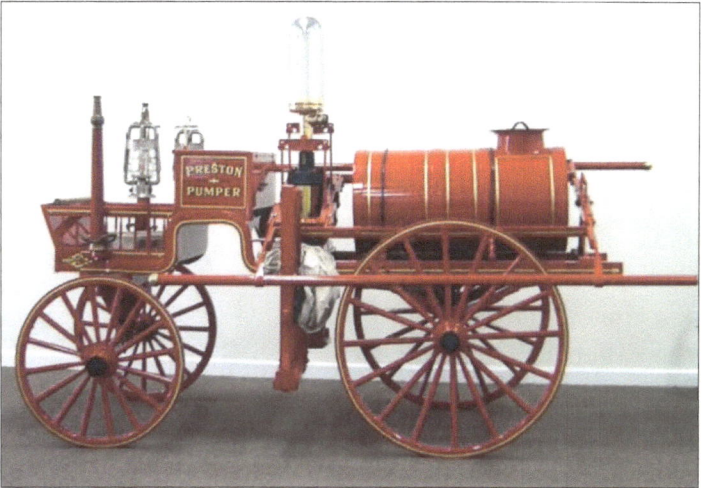

Various Horse Drawn Fire Apparatus once on display in the Gloria Austin Collection. [69]

Pride in the Equipment: Just as today, fire departments took much pride in their equipment. Horse drawn fire apparatus were often decorated with striping, paintings and logos that later evolved into ornate gold leafing and stripes designed to characterize various departments. Lavish paint themes and polished brass added to the glitz, and colors ranged from dark green and brown to maroon, white and red.

Various Fire Bells once on display in the Gloria Austin Collection. [70]

Bells: Prior to horse-drawn fire vehicles, men would run in the streets with bells or bugles to clear the way for the firemen and apparatus. When horses were first used to pull fire vehicles there were already so many tinkling bells on various vehicles in the streets that loud, gong type bells were put on fire vehicles. These were often activated by a foot pedal (right) and mounted on the floor board (left) under the foot pedal.

Sliding Pole: There are conflicting stories and legends about who invented the first fire pole but it is known that in 1880, the Boston Fire Department installed its first brass pole, and it became a standard for fire stations across the United States shortly thereafter. The majority of firehouses in the nineteenth century were two or three stories. Typically, the horse-drawn fire carriages and horses would occupy the first floor, the second floor would be the firefighters' sleeping quarters, and, in some cases, a third floor would serve as a hay bale storage unit to feed the animals. Often, when the firemen cooked meals on the second floor, curious horses would ascend the

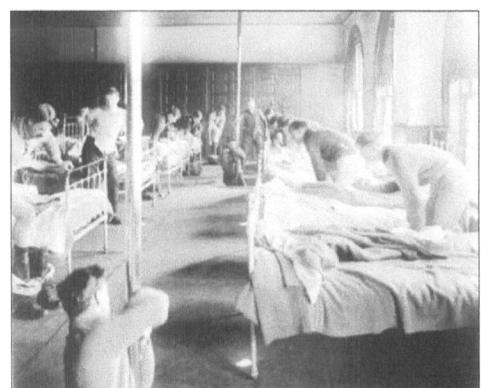

The first Sliding Pole was installed in a Firehouse in 1880. [71]

stairs into the living quarters; as horses typically don't descend stairs, they would then be stuck there. To solve this issue, firehouses began installing narrow spiral staircases that the animals couldn't access. This, however, led to a more pressing issue: when an alarm rang, anywhere from ten to twenty firefighters would all have to simultaneously scramble down these narrow, spiral staircases to reach get below. This invariably impeded response times; in an age where fire technology was limited, every second counted. The firepole saved valuable minutes when the fire alarm bell called firemen to action. (cited from: https://priceonomics.com/the-rise-and-fall-of-the-firemans-pole/)

- *1675 – Great Fire of Northampton, England. The blaze was caused by sparks from an open fire in St. Mary's Street near Northampton castle. In 6 hours it devastated the town centre, destroying about 600 buildings (three-quarters of the town) including All Saints church. 11 people died and about 700 families were made homeless.*
- *1676 – Jamestown, Virginia was burned by Nathaniel Bacon and his followers during Bacon's Rebellion to prevent Governor Berkley from using it as a base.* [177]

- *1677 – Fire of Rostock, Germany, destroys 700 houses and accelerates the city's economic decline at the end of the Hanseatic period.*
- *1678 – Hardegsen. Germany, experienced a fire during the Christmas fair that destroyed most of the town centre. There were no injuries as people were in church.*
- *1684 – Toompea (part of modern Tallinn), a fire destroyed most of the hilltop-town.*
- *1689 – Fire of Skopje of 1689, present-day capital of North Macedonia is burned.*
- *1692 – Two-thirds of Usingen, Germany, is razed, later replaced by a baroque town centre.*
- *1694 – Great Fire of Warwick, England*

Rules and Regulations

In most cities, fire stations were built approximately 2 miles apart to allow for a quick, 5-6 minute response time. The rule excerpts are from the 1901 edition of the "Los Angeles Fire Department Rules and Regulations" and the Daily Routine is from a Los Angeles Fire Department fireman's memoir (courtesy of the LAFD Historical Society).

RULE 11. HOUSE AND HOUSE WATCH.

SECTION 1. The telephones in the houses shall not be used by any person not a member of the Department, nor by any member or employee for any other business than that connected with the Department.

SEC. 2. Thorough ventilation should be maintained in the houses, avoiding draughts as much as possible.

SEC. 3. Houses should be thoroughly washed and scrubbed at least once a month, weather permitting.

SEC. 4. A house watch shall be maintained in all houses of the Department between the hours of 6.00 A.M. and 8 P.M., and during the entire 24 hours in such houses as the Chief Engineer may order.

SEC. 5. It shall be the duty of the man on watch to be on the lookout for alarms, to see that the apparatus, horses, harness and everything appertaining thereto is in good order and ready for immediate service. That no disturbances are allowed in or about the house, and report any and all violations of these Rules and Regulations in or about the house to the commanding officer of the company.

SEC. 6. In no case shall the man on watch leave the apparatus floor until relived, except in case of an alarm; nor shall he doze or sleep while on watch. (above: LA Engine Co No 1, No 2, No 3, No 4)

Engine Company No. 1
1901 Pasadena Ave. & Ave. 19,
East Los Angeles [72]

Engine Company No. 2
2127 East First Street
Boyle Heights [73]

Engine Company No. 3
346-348 South Hill Street [74]

Engine Company No. 4
227 Aliso Street
near Los Angeles Street [75]

RULE 33
DAILY HITCH UPS

SECTION 1. It shall be the duty of the members of a company to hitch the horses to the apparatus daily at 8.00 A.M., 12 Noon and 5.00 P.M.; and all snaps, trips and appliances pertaining to the harness must be released the same as when there is an alarm. There will be no hitch-ups on Sundays or legal holidays.

Engine 23, 1915, Los Angeles, CA. [76]

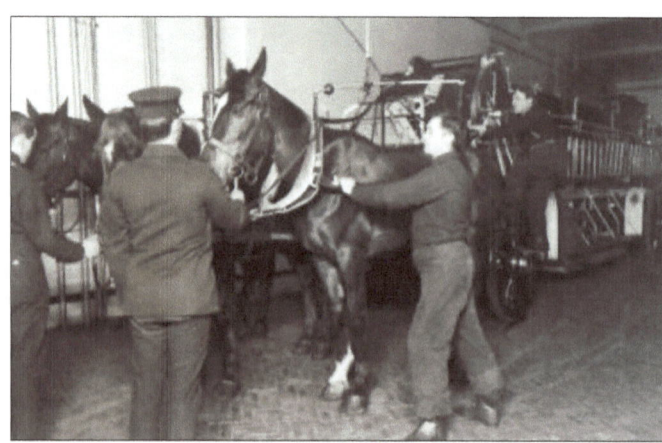

Hitching up the fire horses, 1906. [65]

- *1696 – St. John's, Newfoundland, and 35 other settlements were burned by French forces under Pierre Le Moyne d'Iberville.*
- *1702 – Uppsala, Sweden, devastated in large part and the cathedral and Uppsala Castle severely damaged.* [178]

- *1702 – Bergen, at the time the largest city in Norway, seven-eighths destroyed during a storm.*
- *1707 – Xàtiva, the second most important city in the former Kingdom of Valencia, was burnt down as an exemplary punishment by the Bourbon king Philip V of Spain after besieging and conquering it.*
- *1711 – Great Boston Fire of 1711. Destroyed the First Town-House*
- *1726 – Reutlingen, Germany, Free Imperial City, 80% of all residential houses and almost all public buildings destroyed, making 1,200 families homeless.*
- *1728 – Copenhagen Fire of 1728, Denmark, two-fifths of the city burned down during three days. 3,650 families became homeless.*
- *1731 – Blandford Forum, Dorset, England, a large majority of the town was destroyed on 4 June. The aftermath of this fire had an Act of Parliament passed stating that rebuilding work must be in brick and tile.*

KING STREET FIRE STATION 1929-30

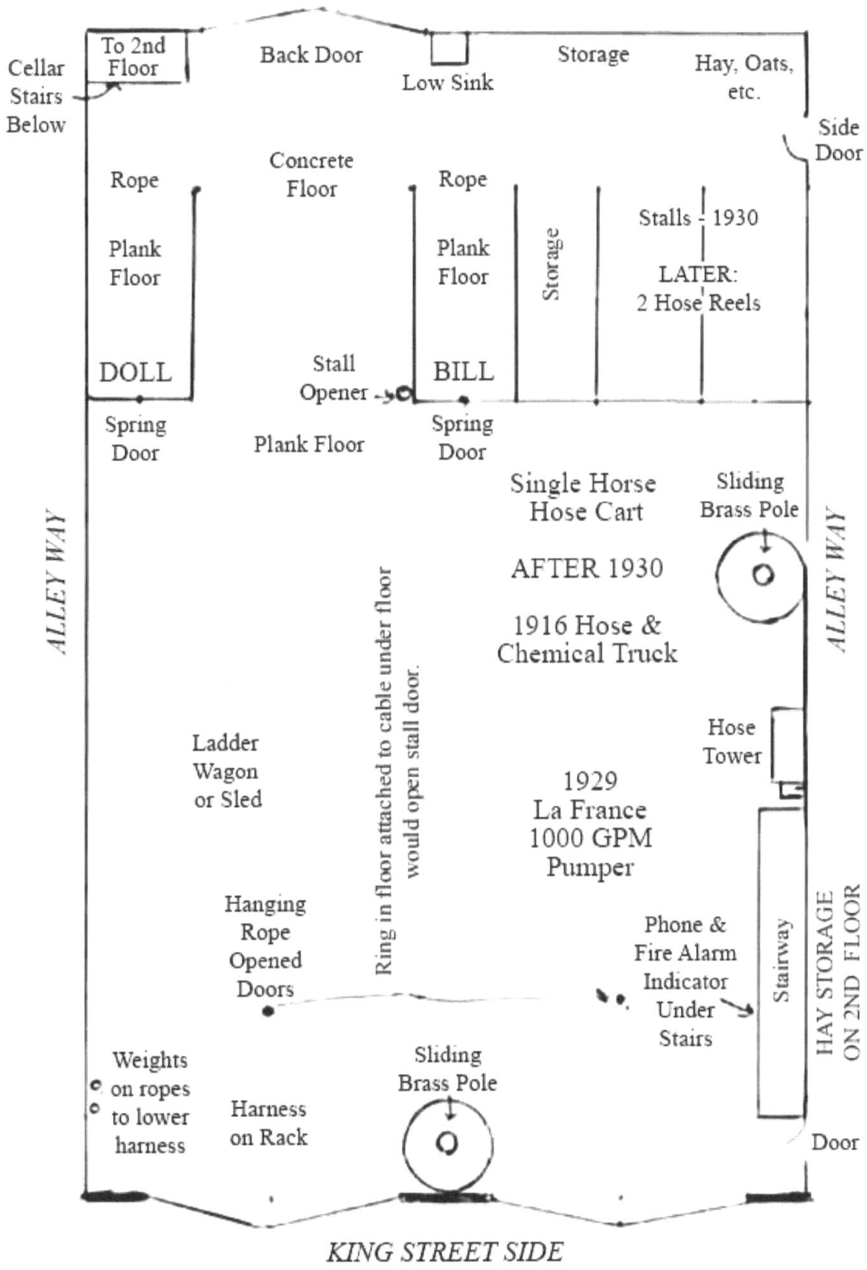

(Floor plan labels:)
- Cellar Stairs Below
- To 2nd Floor
- Back Door
- Low Sink
- Storage
- Hay, Oats, etc.
- Side Door
- Rope / Plank Floor — DOLL
- Concrete Floor
- Rope / Plank Floor — BILL
- Stall Opener
- Storage
- Stalls – 1930 / LATER: 2 Hose Reels
- Spring Door
- Plank Floor
- Spring Door
- Single Horse Hose Cart / AFTER 1930 / 1916 Hose & Chemical Truck
- Sliding Brass Pole
- ALLEY WAY (both sides)
- Ladder Wagon or Sled
- Ring in floor attached to cable under floor would open stall door.
- 1929 La France 1000 GPM Pumper
- Hose Tower
- Hanging Rope Opened Doors
- Phone & Fire Alarm Indicator Under Stairs
- Stairway
- HAY STORAGE ON 2ND FLOOR
- Weights on ropes to lower harness
- Harness on Rack
- Sliding Brass Pole
- Door
- KING STREET SIDE

All vehicles, harnesses and apparatus were ready to go at all times. (above: floor plan of Frederiction Firehouse) Horses wore their bits all day except when eating.

- *1731 – Tiverton fire, Devon, England, burned nearly 300 houses. Rumored to start in a bakers house. Photo depicts firehooks. Firehooks are used to help tear down buildings to stop fires from spreading as seen during a fire at Tiverton in Devon, England, 1612.* [179]

- *1734 – Montreal, New France*
- *1752 – Fire destroys 18,000 houses in Moscow, 5–6 May.*
- *1754 – The Great Fire of Hindon swept through the village of Hindon, Wiltshire, burning 144 houses and buildings to the ground.*
- *1759 – The Second Great Stockholm Fire (Swedish: Mariabranden meaning brand = fire) in Södermalm, Stockholm, Sweden, destroyed about 300 buildings.*
- *1760 – Fire in the town of Porvoo, Finland (then part of Sweden) burned down most of the settlement on June 11. Propagated by long drought and strong wind.*
- *1760 – Great Boston Fire of 1760, 349 buildings destroyed*
- *1775 – Great Fire of Tartu, Estonia, nearly 200 buildings destroyed*

The job of the driver was the most prestigious. They were responsible for the horses and the horse tack. It was the highest paid position but also the most difficult and often times, dangerous.

RULE 8.
DRIVERS.

SECTION 1. Drivers shall take proper care of their horses, exercise the greatest caution in their keeping and management, keep the stalls clean, and see that everything pertaining to the horses, harness, hangers, etc., is in perfect order and ready at all times for immediate service.

SEC. 2. Drivers of hose apparatus will precede the other apparatus of the Company in responding to alarms, unless otherwise directed by the Chief Engineer.

SEC. 3. In returning from an alarm, all driving shall be at a moderate rate of speed.

SEC. 4. Drivers shall not pass a fire to take a hydrant, unless by so doing they can obtain a closer position to the fire without shutting out another company that may be seen or is known to be coming from another direction.

SEC. 5. Driver of trucks, chemicals, etc., must not stop their apparatus in front of a hydrant.

SEC. 6. They shall not drive their apparatus over hose except when absolutely necessary. Driver of hose apparatus will lay their hose close to the curb of the street as possible.

A turn of the century horse-drawn steamer races to a fire, with fireman Al Lambla at the reins. [78]

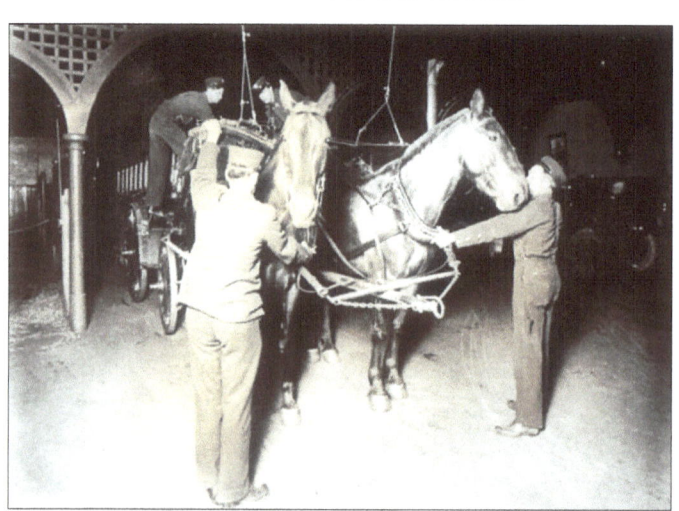

Driver climbs abroad as firemen readying the horses at Fire Company No. 1., San Diego Fire Department. [79]

The Daily Routine

A fireman started at the salary of $75 a month, working 24 hours a day, seven days a week, the meal hours ran in three periods, as follows, divided up in shifts from 6 a.m. to 9 a.m. for breakfast, and so on until supper time. You could take three one-hour meals, or two one and a half ones, or one three-hour meal. Anyway, if you had a family you only saw them three hours a day. Hardly enough for your wife and children to know you.

Recreation floor, Engine 23, 1915, Los Angeles, CA. [80]

The Driver: of horse drawn apparatus and officers usually had the first meal hour. As the drivers arose at 5 a.m. their first duty was to water horses out of a bucket, give them a feed of rolled barley, pick up the bedding of straw from under the horses, put it in a box on rollers, wheel it outside quarters, then hit the pole or ring the bell to get up the rest of the company, who were on the apparatus floor for taps and roll call at 6 a.m. After which, all the men turned to and swept the apparatus floor. In some companies the horses were hitched up and the apparatus was driven out on the street for exercise of the horses for one hour. As the driver returned he had to curry the horses all over, wash out mouths, clean teeth, hoofs and polish halters, flush out stalls, give the animals a feed of bran at noon, at night bed them down, and give them a feed of barley hay.

Fireman on house watch, New York. NY. 1906. [81]

Floor Watch: stood from 6 a.m. to 8 p.m. The duty of the man on watch was to keep the floor of the stall where the horses stood clear of all matter, etc. You were always kept busy, unloading hay, briquets, grain, coal, and kindling. As every fire alarm box pulled in any part of the city came in to all fire houses it was necessary at night to get up many times and yet not respond to any alarms. If an alarm and a go, there was a mad scramble to run out into the street and get on the apparatus. In two story houses it was a continuation of sliding the pole and then walking back up the stairs. After every alarm there was roll call with all names being checked off in the journal. Upon returning to quarters after a fire run, the Engineer put in new excelsior, kindling and coal to be ready for the next alarm. You can see that if you responded to a number of calls how busy the engineer was, in fact all the boys. You did not in those days pile into bed upon return to quarters from a fire.

Chemical tanks: if used at a fire, needed to be refilled and the chemical hose needed to be washed out. Sometimes these tanks were dumped more than once at night and you can see the hours put in and loss of sleep. The axels of the apparatus had to be jacked up once a month and greased. The traveling horse shoeing wagon with a horse shoer and helper came to the station once a month to shoe the horses. If a horse got sick the Vet Doctor was called, and if too sick another horse had to be brought from the corral at Ave. 19 and Pasadena Ave.

Then as now, firefighters spent at least as much time inside the firehouse as actually fighting fires. Occasional visits from celebrities, like opera singer Nellie Melba (Downton Abbey fans may remember an episode which featured a performance by Dame Melba at Downton!) were among the perks of the job. Fire Chief Edward F. Croker and opera singer Madam Nellie Melba (below) inspecting Engine Co. 65 in New York City, 1910 (cited from: http://blog.nyhistory.org/what-the-business-requires-images/). In case you never heard of her, she was colossal at the time – so much so that that Melba Toast and Peach Melba were created in her name by famed chef Auguste Escoffier. A visit to a firehouse by a celebrity would have been a very incredible event at the time; to the horses though (background), it's just another day at the firehouse.

Fire Chief Edward F. Croker and opera singer Madam Nellie Melba inspecting Engine Co. 65, 1910. [82]

- **1776 – First Great Fire of New York City of 1776.** [180]

- **1776 – Around two-thirds of Varaždin, the capital of Croatia at the time, destroyed in a fire of unknown origin.**
- **1787 – Great Boston Fire of 1787. 100 buildings destroyed in the southern part of Boston.**
- **1788 – First Great New Orleans Fire of 1788, 856 out of 1,100 structures burned.**
- **1788 – Great Fire of Tenmei, Kyoto, Japan, 150 killed, 37,000 houses burned, on March 6.**
- **1793 – Cap Français (modern-day Cap-Haïtien, Haiti).** [181]

- **1794 – Second Great New Orleans Fire of 1794, 212 structures destroyed.**
- **1795 – Copenhagen fire of 1795**
- **1805 – Great Fire of 1805: Detroit, Michigan Territory, then a wooden frontier settlement, burned except for a river warehouse.**

The Sound of the Alarm

One of the drawbacks of the steam engine was the time it took to generate steam from cold water. To solve this, a heater, usually in the basement, was connected by pipes to the steamers. The heater circulated hot water in the boiler coils of the steamer. A damper fitted over the stack helped to keep the water hot. Preheated water enabled steamers to start pumping in less than 3 minutes or less after arriving at a fire. At first horses were kept in the barn outside of the station but getting the horses out took valuable time. Eventually, horses moved into the firehouse and stalls were located at the rear or sides of the apparatus. The apparatus floor was austere with only the watchman on duty. His job was to regularly check the hot water on the steamer, look in on the horses and be alert for alarms.

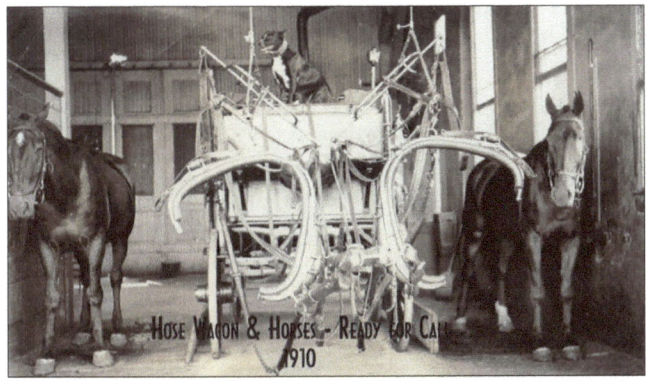

Hose, wagon, and horses ready for call in 1910. [63]

THE ALARM SOUNDS!

At the first clang of the gong the men slid down the pole and the station doors opened, lights came on and stall doors were automatically released. The trained horses trotted to their apparatus and backed into position under their harness – they were in position before all of the men were down the pole! The engineer lifted the damper, flipped a match into the boiler furnace, ignited the wood shavings or kerosene-soaked cotton waste. Some firehouses had burning gas jets in the floor which ignited the kindling when the engine passed over them. As the steamer started ahead the coupling to the hot water heater snapped apart and a clapper valve automatically shut off the flow. Most companies could leave the station in 45 seconds!

Firemen ready the horses.

At every alarm, go or not, the harness had to be dropped over the horses. The driver hooked the harness on the horse on his side and another man hooked the harness on the horse on the other side. It was necessary to grab the collar that hung over the horse, pull it down over the horse's neck and snap the collar, grab the reins that hung on the collar, and snap them to the bridle that was always on the horse. If it was a no go, it was necessary to unsnap the reins, unhook the collar and hang everything back on the hook, and push it up and out of the way; then take the horse back to the stall. This was a continuous process.

The engineer who rode on the rear of the steam engine had a time keeping from being thrown off in responding to alarms, as the wheels of the drawn engine had steel tires and skidded all over the streets. The driver of the engine, upon arriving at a fire, had to unhitch the horses, take them some distance from the engine and tie them up. Drivers of the hose wagon and the engine were strapped to their seats. It was a thrill to see the horses plunging at full speed to a fire, giving their best, and they were beloved by the men at the stations. The engineer had the duty of building fires in the fire boxes of the steam engines, which was as follows: First a layer of excelsior, then kindling, then some coal.

Snapping the collar onto the firehorses.

When an alarm came in he was to light a coal oil torch on the engine which he lighted up the fire in the fire box. Some engineers thought up a better idea. They had a contrivance under the fire box which held a mixture of sugar and potash. Near it was a bottle of acid. As the response to the alarm was made, a chain pulled by the engineer broke the bottle of acid, causing it to mix with the potash and a flame was ignited in the excelsior. In a few moments steam was raised and sometimes the engineer had the stoker or fireman shovel coal into the fire box at the fire; and those fire boxes ate the coal! To hear the even exhaust of the engine and see sparks and smoke flying out of the stack was a thrill. When coal was needed a shrill blast on the steam whistle at the engine called the coal wagon to come. The engineer had his troubles if the boiler foamed. His eyes were on the water glass at the boiler and pressure gauge at all times.

In 1860, the city of Detroit purchased its first steam-powered firefighting equipment. It had a pumping capacity of 600 gallons a minute and was pulled to fires by two horses. Records show it cost $3,150. This steam engine is shown in an undated photo. [83]

The driver was always strapped in the seat. The engineer had a coal torch on the back of the engine that he lit when responding and then lit fire in firebox, which was laid with excelsior and kindling, with some coal on top. The tires on hose wagon and engine were of steel and apparatus on way to fires slid and swung all over the street. The engineer on arriving at fires had to shovel coal into the firebox besides his other duties. A coal wagon responded to fires to supply coal for engines, and when engines were working, the streets were filled with smoke from the stacks, as some engines ate the coal as fast as you could shovel it in the firebox. Boilers foamed sometimes causing more work for the engineers.

Driver strapped in on a Hook & Ladder Truck No. 1, El Paso, Texas. [86]

Engineer with steam engine. Chicago. 1902. [84]

Hose Wagon on its way to the Triangle Shirtwaist Company fire, New York City, 1911. [91]

Engine 5 at 1906 Manhattan Ribbon Fire - On Arch Street bridge. [85]

Watching the shining steamers speeding down the streets behind galloping horses was thrilling. Smoke, sparks, gongs and horses racing to the fires – how thrilling to watch! Frequently scores of youngsters, running and on bikes, followed the engines.

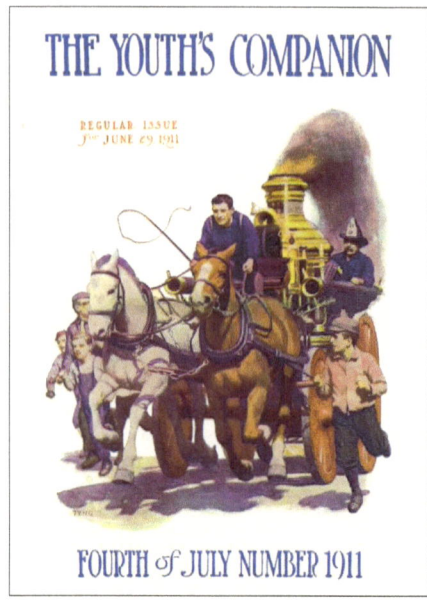

Regular issue for June 29, 1911 of The Youth's Companion. [87]

Firemen riding horse-drawn steam powered fire engine down city street; crowds gather to watch. Wausau, Wisconsin, 1913. [88]

Engine Co. 205, New York, NY, 1922. [90]

Fire horses in action, Winthrop, MA, 1917–1934. [89]

It was indeed thrilling to watch but often dangerous too! Horses galloped at full speed through the congested traffic, often on slippery streets. They had to navigate trolley tracks, mud, ice, snow and tight corners. Often there were turnovers, slips and falls and, with the rise in automobile numbers, there was increased danger.

Steam Pumper, 1905. [97]

Engine 22's Horse-drawn steam pumper, 1900. [93]

Hose 5 on runners, 1920. [92]

Horse-drawn Steam Engine at intersection of West 43rd Street and Broadway, New York City, 1910 -1915. [94]

Horse-drawn Steam Pumper Accident. Laurium MI, 1928. [94]

"Most of the streets were unpaved, making it easier for the horses to get a footing. On pavement the animals were likely to fall on turns. They did fall and tip the engine over at Fourth and C St.." — Clarence Woodson. 1913. [96]

As cities spread and fire districts grew, chiefs could no longer run to fires. Soon there arrived a new apparatus in the fire department fleet – the chief's buggy. Some stations provided an apartment on site for the chief and his family. Other stations kept the wagon close to the chief's house and when the alarm went off, a driver would pick up the chief and take him to the fire. It was commonplace in larger cities to have extra horses at firehouses. When the chief's horse was winded, he would stop at a station and pick up another horse; much like a Pony Express run!

Hotel Street Firehouse with gig of Chief John Stagg and driver George Pfitzenmeyer, 1900. New Jersey. [99]

Horse-Drawn Chief's Buggy, with Assistant Chief of Department - Ralph Cook, 1900. Seattle, WA. [98]

During the long hours at the fire, horses were required to stand patiently despite the heat, flames, sparks, flying glass, steamer smoke, whistles, bells, more galloping horses arriving, yelling men, screaming people, crashing walls, icy spray in their faces and milling spectators.

Horses on duty, protected from floating embers with blankets at a fire. [102]

The team pulling the ladder wagon waiting calmly. 1900. [100]

Fire at close range, Whart St. Boston, MA. 1916. [101]

Fire men and their fire dog [103]

First Bay Saranac Lake Firehouse, New York. [104]

Dogs often traveled with the fire departments to stay with the horses in order to guard them. Most stations had mutts but Dalmatians were often seen. When the fire department left the station in route to a fire, the dogs were the first out the door, barking at people in the road to move them to safety. Once the wagon was in the road and rolling to the fire, the dogs would make sure the wagon never had to stop for pedestrians. Dogs were the first sirens. Once they arrived, there was still the matter of the fire and how the horses reacted to it. Often fire is scary for animals, but the presence of the dogs would ease the stress of the situation on the horses. Guarding the wagon was another job they had once the fire department arrived, can you imagine that people would steal from the guys trying to save lives? Well, they wouldn't with these guys around! (cited from: https://3milliondogs.com/dogbook/how-dalmatians-became-the-firehouse-mascot/)

Jiggs, the long-time coach dog and mascot of Engine Company No. 205 howled in sorrow as his horse friends were bid their final farewell. [101]

Fire department mascot Bozo gets a hug from Frank Noonan. Detroit, 1929. Dog mascots were banned in 1976, over concerns that they might frighten citizens and prompt lawsuits. [102]

Water Sources: Steamers needed to keep pumping through the duration of the fire. As was mentioned previously, during the Great San Francisco fire, there were so many steam engines working that the pressure pulled the wooden water mains right out of the ground. In New York City the Croton Aqueduct had supplied water to New York City hydrants since 1842, and the fire department supplemented the Croton supply with water from the river. But as the city grew, available water pressure was insufficient to reach the new skyscrapers that were rapidly becoming part of the urban landscape and it became clear that high-pressure water delivery was needed to fight fires in a vertical city. Between 1903 and 1908, 4 new high-pressure pumping stations were constructed, 2 in Brooklyn and 2 in Manhattan. In response to alarms, these stations would increase the water pressure threefold or more and send it through high-pressure mains to fire hydrants, where the trucks would tap into it. The Gansevoort Station had 5 pumps, each of which could deliver 2,700 gallons per minute.
(cited from: http://blog.nyhistory.org/what-the-business-requires-images/)

Hydrant hooked to a Steam Engine at a fire. First Bay Saranac Lake Firehouse, New York. The boiler produced steam, which created a vacuum in the 2,000 lb. steamer and enabled firemen to suck water from a reservoir or other source through the steamer to be shot up under pressure into the fire hoses. This enabled firemen to fight multi-story fires from the street for the first time. [104]

Interior of Gansevoort Street High Pressure Pumping Station, New York, 1910. [105]

High-Pressure Pumping System test, West & Bank Streets, New York, 1908. [106]

If the horses were warm on return from a response it was necessary to walk them until they cooled off.

H. Heinzelman, C. Kennedy, J. Eagan, Wm Smith and horses of Engine Company 4, New Jersey, 1911-12. [108]

Paterson, New Jersey Fire Department with horses and walking horses, New Jersey. [107]

The engineer, after returning from a fire, had to work filling the oiler, greasing and getting the engine ready for the next run. (information in this section courtesy of LAFD Historical Society cited from: http://www.lafire.com/stations/fire_stations.htm and also cited from: Ditzel, Paul C. (1976) Fire Engines Firefighters: The Men, Equipment, and Machines, from Colonial Days to the Present. New York, New York. Rutledge Books. Pp 127-135)

Steam Fire Engine No. 8, 1909. Grand Rapids Fire Department. Kalamazoo, MI. [109]

Types of Horses

Horses had to be strong, as well as fast and surefooted to pull apparatus, weighing several tons, along streets sometimes slickened by rain, sleet or snow. Galloping at full speed, they had to work with single minded concentration as a finely tuned team responding to the orders of the driver. More went into selecting fire horses than selecting firemen! Many eastern fire departments went deep into the Midwest to buy the very best. Mares, stallions and geldings were all used. Teams of 2 and 3 horses were matched for size and sometimes, although not important, for color.

Hose Wagon [110]

The Detroit Fire Department specified sizes for the various apparatus: 1,100 pounds for hose wagon teams, 1,400 pounds for steamer teams and 1,700 pounds for hook and ladder teams. According to the Detroit Fire Department, "To be an ideal Fire Department horse the animal must possess exceptional intelligence, an even, yet strong, temperament, tractability, perfection of body, limb and wind, and the required weight." During that time, the description of what was needed to be a fireman was much the same, but with one omission.... there was no mention of exceptional intelligence.
(cited from: Ditzel, Paul C. (1976) Fire Engines Firefighters: The Men, Equipment, and Machines, from Colonial Days to the Present. New York, New York. Rutledge Books. Pp 135-136)

Steamer teams [35]

Hook and Ladder teams [111]

The question became how to pick or breed the best horses for the job. To find potential fire horses, authorities searched for horses that were fast, strong, agile, obedient, fearless and able to stand calm and patient in difficult circumstances, in all kinds of weather. Morgans were often used as horses for Fire Chiefs and Percheron or Percheron crosses were most often used for the apparatus. In Portland, Oregon, Percheron-Morgan hybrids were bred that would have the power to pull the heavy engines through the muddy streets and get them to the fire on time. (cited from: Levin, Jonathon V. (2017) Where Have All the Horse Gone? Jefferson, North Carolina. McFarland & Company, Inc. P. 98)

The great Percheron stallion, Leon, with owner Harry Stamp

The Percheron has a very pleasing disposition. He is proud, alert, intelligent and a willing worker. They range in height from 15 to 19 hands high and can weigh up to 2600 pounds with the average around 1900 pounds. Percherons are noted for heavy muscling in the lower thighs and for an aspect of unusual ruggedness and power. The Percheron is very versatile. They are readily adapted to varying climates and conditions. They have the strength to pull heavy loads. He is also expected to be of marked tractability and an easy keeper. (cited from: https://www.percheronhorse.org/percheron-disposition-and-characteristics/)

The great Morgan stallion, Ulendon, with Dr. Wallace Orcutt

The beauty of the Morgan horse lifts the heart. The breed exists solely because they want to please. The height ranges from 14.1 to 15.2 hands with some individuals over or under. They should be compact with a short back, close coupling, broad loins, deep flank, well-sprung ribs, croup long and well-muscled. Morgans are known for their stamina, vigor, alertness, adaptability, attitude and tractability. Reliable, loyal, tireless, and versatile, a Morgan becomes one with people. It's their heritage. (cited from: https://www.morganhorse.com)

Care and Training of Horses

The Detroit Fire Department Legacy was very helpful in providing information for this section. Most horses in fire departments had "on the job" training. In the firehouse, horses were trained to respond to the alarm by repeating the process of ringing the alarm, putting the horse in position and putting on the harness. Horses were teamed with experienced horses when it came time to pull apparatus. Detroit however, had a "Horse College" to train and care for their horses; the horse college was well known and widely respected!

The "on the job" training method was not always the best. In 1887, Allen Armstrong, Superintendent of Horses for the Detroit Fire Department wrote in the Annual Report of the Fire Commission of Detroit that, "The present system for training new horses should be changed. An animal new to the business is placed alongside a veteran to be taught to run out at the sound of the gong. He can be made to leave his stall in a very short time but the excitement, the sight of the bright work on the apparatus frighten him, and often times a really good horse for the business is spoiled in the training. I think it would be a measure of economy to establish a training stable remote from the engine house." (cited from: Annual Report of the Controller of the City of Detroit, fiscal year ending June 30, 1887) Thus the "horse college" in Detroit was established.

Allen Armstrong, December 1890. Superintendent of Horses. [112]

In July 1886 the department established a Horse Bureau with Allen A. Armstrong appointed as Superintendent. Superintendent was a rank equivalent to Battalion Chief. Armstrong had been employed as foreman of the Detroit Omnibus Line and had previously been a member of Detroit's volunteer hand engine company "Neptune 2". He was selected by the Fire Commission for this position because he had a thorough knowledge of horses and their ailments. In this position Armstrong devoted his entire time to the care of horses. His responsibilities included regulating of feeding and exercise, supervising shoeing, regulating the training of the newly purchased horses and ensuring the horses were properly cared for and handled. (information courtesy of DFD Legacy)

Allen Armstrong, Supt. of Horses. [115]

Superintendent Armstrong was instrumental in getting the department to build a dedicated horse facility (in 1889) and developing a horse training school, the first of its kind in the nation. It was located at Russell & Calhoun (now Erskine) Streets, behind Ladder 5's quarters. The new facilities allowed for the horses to be eased into training away from the commotion of the engine house. The Training Stables consisted of a brick single-story supply stable building that contained box and open stalls for 25 horses. A 2-story wooden building housed a training room and various rooms for storage of equipment and feed. The training room, fitted up like an engine house, was used for training new horses. Next to the stables was a 14' wide, 700' long cinder track which allowed the new horses to get used to pulling department apparatus at speeds similar to those required when responding to an alarm. The department's sick and injured horses were also cared for at this facility and extra horses were also housed here. Additionally, the shoeing of all the department's horses was done here. Between 1890 and 1892 the staff of the stables consisted of Superintendent Armstrong, Driver Charles Little and 3 grooms. In 1893, 2 additional grooms were added. Charles Little was one of the firemen who went to Chicago to help fight the Great Chicago Fire of 1871.

Chief Martin Cooney, Supt. of Horses, 1880. Detroit Fire Dept. [113]

Chemical Company No. 6. The foremost driver is Martin Cooney, who would later become superintendent of horses, 1891. [114]

Superintendent of Horses Allen Armstrong died from heart failure and pneumonia on November 13, 1893. When Armstrong died the responsibilities of Superintendent of Horses were assigned to William J. Gowan. Gowan was the department's Chief of the 2nd Battalion, in which the training stables were located. In August, 1894 Martin Cooney was named Assistant Superintendent of Horses. Cooney was an experienced horseman and driver in the department.

Chief Gowan was responsible for overseeing the activities of the Training Stables while Cooney did the actual hands on work with the horses. In 1894 the Fire Commission learned, through reading about it in a local newspaper, of a proposition to take the land that the Training Stables and track was located on and convert it into storage lots for the city's water commission. The Commission pleaded its case to City Council that taking away the department's training facility without first providing an alternate facility would paralyze the fire department. Commissioners pointed out that Detroit was the first to adapt their advanced methods of training and all prominent cities have since endorsed it. They pointed out that going back to the old ways with the horses would be a great mistake and loosing these training grounds would handicap the department beyond expression. Fortunately, the plan was abandoned, and the department's horse training facilities remained at this location. By 1897 the stables had been extended to run all the way down the property line extending from the building housing the training room to the corner of Benton Avenue. There were now stables for 35 horses.

In September 1899 Superintendent of Horses Gowan passed away. Martin Cooney, who had been Assistant Superintendent, was promoted to fill his position and the position of Assistant Superintendent was done away with. The Assistant Superintendent's position was brought back in 1901. In 1905 a brick building replaced the original wooden building of the training stables. The building was designed by Architects John Scott & Company, built by I. E. Boomer at a cost of $11,766. The new brick two-story building housed a hay loft, sleeping rooms, a small office in the upper level and a training room below. In 1905 the Horse Bureau added an additional grooms position. Personnel now consisted of: Superintendent Cooney, Assistant Superintendent John McLaughlin, and 6 grooms. By 1914 personnel had expanded once again. There were now 8 grooms. In 1917 a new Assistant Superintendent, Frank E. Stocks, was appointed. Superintendent Cooney retired later that year. His position was filled by Chief Hugh Peters. Both Peters and Stock remained in these positions until the last running of the fire horses in April 1922. Assistant Superintendent Stock retired on the same day as his beloved fire horses. Chief Peters continued with the department in another capacity.

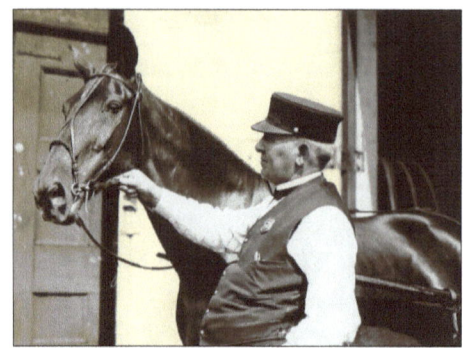

Martin Cooney, Superintendent of Horses, D.F.D., 1910. [116]

For 27 years Martin Cooney was superintendent of horses for the fire department of Detroit. He bought every horse used by the department in that time and he tended them through sickness. So great was his love for horses that he never took a furlough, or even kept his Sundays for himself. Night and day, he watched over the horses. In winter, when the horses, steaming from their swift run to the fires, it was Martin Cooney who hurried to the scene, and saw that they were blanketed. Back in their barns, it was Martin Cooney who saw that they were rubbed down and made warm and comfortable. When their feet were sore it was Martin Cooney who dressed them, and when the strenuous life of a fire department horse made them unfit for further service, Martin Cooney saw to it that they were sold to farmers and

- *1807 – The Second Battle of Copenhagen led to the burning of over a thousand buildings in the city, including the Church of Our Lady.*
- *1811 – Great Fire of Podil in Kiev, Russian Empire. Over 2,000 buildings, 12 churches and 3 abbeys destroyed; about 30 deaths.*
- *1812 – The Fire of Moscow of 1812 was burned to deny shelter to Napoleon.*
- *1812–1814 – The War of 1812 involved several major urban fires:*
- *1813 – Buffalo, New York*
- *1813 – York, Upper Canada*
- *1814 – Burning of Washington*
- *1813 – Portsmouth, New Hampshire*
- *1814 – Great fire of Tirschenreuth in Tirschenreuth, Bavaria, totally destroys the town apart from the parish church and 3 neighboring buildings.* [182]

- *1817 – St. John's, Newfoundland*
- *1820 – Ponce, Puerto Rico, a Spanish settlement, was almost completely destroyed on February 27.*
- *1820 – Great Savannah Fire burned almost 500 structures, with damages of about $4 million.*
- *1821 – Paramaribo, Suriname, fire destroyed over 400 houses.*
- *1821 – Great Fire of Fayetteville destroyed 500 buildings in the city.*

not to city drivers who might abuse them. (cited from: Our Dumb Animals, Volume 50, No. 1, June 1917)

For the first several years of horse drawn fire apparatus, Detroit Fire Department fire horses were cared for by the drivers of the company they were assigned to under the direction of that company's foreman. When an injury was sustained that required specialized care an outside person was paid on a per case basis. It is uncertain if the outside people hired were simply knowledgeable horsemen or trained veterinary surgeons. On August 1, 1864 the department's supply wagon driver, William J. Wolf, took on the added responsibilities of caring for sick or injured horses. The supply wagon responded to every fire and would carry extra coal and hose to steamers while at a fire scene. Wolf was not schooled in veterinary sciences but was a well-respected horseman. He was the department's first paid driver when the first steam engine was placed in service. Supply wagon driver/veterinary officer was the department's 2nd highest paid full-time firefighter making $75 per month. (chief, foremen, pipemen and laddermen were still part time) Engineers who ran and serviced the steam pumpers, were the only higher paid personnel, paid $5 per month more.

Detroit Fire Department Engine Company 4 on Orchard and Fifth, built 1865. [117]

On June 16, 1873 the department's first veterinary surgeon, John C. Gregory, was appointed to care for the horses. He was required to visit and inspect all horses twice a week. It's interesting to note that the department appointed a department veterinarian two months before it appointed a department doctor to care for the men. Good horses were harder to find than good men.

Detroit Fire Department Engine Company 5 on Alexandrine near Cass, built in 1876. [118]

By mid-1878 the department stopped employing a department veterinary surgeon. Instead they established a "Supply Stable" on Orchard Street, between 5th and 6th. The department's extra horses and sick or injured hoses were kept there under the care of a competent horseman who was a member of the department.

In 1882, with the department expanding, a department horse infirmary was established at Engine 5's quarters, Alexandrine near Cass Avenue. The sick and injured horses were cared for by Robert Jennings one of the most experienced drivers in the department, who devoted his entire time to this care. When a horse would become unfit for service, he was sent to the infirmary where, after removing his shoes. he was placed in a large box stall. The horse would remain there until he was again fit for the strenuous duty of fire department service. In addition to sick and injured horses this location also housed new and extra horses.

The following excerpt is from: *Our Firemen: A Record of the Faithful and Heroic Men Who Guard the Property and Live in the City of Detroit and a Review of the Past.* It was edited by Charles Hathaway in 1894 and issued for the benefit of the Fireman's Fund Association. It is an excellent description of the Horse College in Detroit. The Detroit Fire Department's Horse College was widely respected throughout the United States.

The horses of the Detroit Fire Department—180 in number—are under the supervision of Battalion Chief Wm. J. Gowan, who assigns the horses to the several companies, changing them from place to place as circumstances may require; for as a horse may work well in one house and refuse to do duty in another, it is necessary at times to remove him from quarters that are not congenial to a home that suits his tastes. The Department Horse Bureau was established in 1886, with Allen Armstrong as Superintendent, who, after long and most successful service, was succeeded by Chief Gowan, who is eminently fitted for the position. The Superintendent of Horses is governed by regulations prescribing his duties, and his work is done under the supervision of the Committee on Horses. The chairman of this committee is Commissioner Fred. T. Moran, who has occupied the position for several years, and it is no exaggeration when the credit of the present exceptionally choice horse equipment of the Detroit Fire Department is awarded to that gentleman. His thorough knowledge as to horses, and his zeal and pride in the affairs of the Department, have proved invaluable.

In selecting horses for the Department, young and sound animals are the only prerequisites, as their adaptability can only be determined after they have been trained. This training and the general care of the animals, including the feeding and shoeing, is regulated by the Superintendent, who also attends the sick and injured animals, and has power to summon a veterinary surgeon when necessary. No horse is bought unless up to the standard weight.

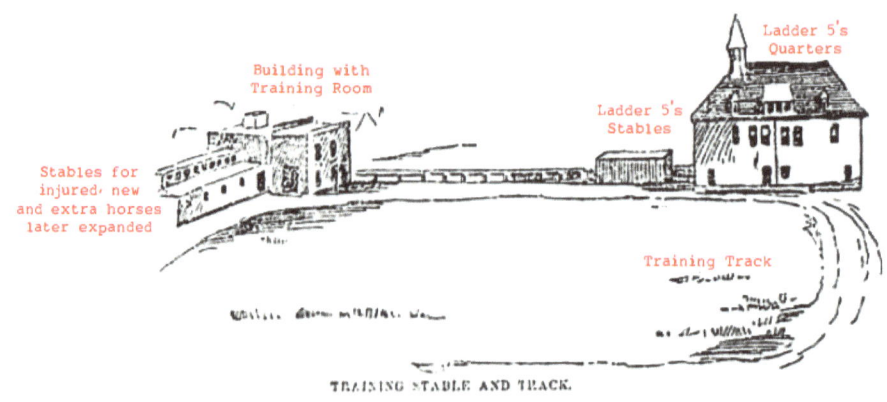

Engine Co. 5 home of the Horse College

Long experience proved that it was poor policy to continue the general practice of placing new horses here and there, to be trained by different drivers. Accordingly, in 1882, a number of box stalls were built in rear of engine house No. 5, and all new or disabled horses were quartered there, the men of that company being assigned to their training. (above: Engine Co 5 home of the horse college) Again, was a lesson taught by experience. It was that horses in training required exact conditions to produce the best results. For instance, a country bred horse, unused, even, to paved streets, would be placed behind an engine, in a stall by the side of an old

timer. The gong would strike, the trip would fall, the doors would fly open, and as the veteran would rush out to his place the new horse would follow, but the "chug chug" of the heater, the glitter of the bright work on the apparatus, and the shouts and efforts of the men as they tried to push him under the harness, set his nerves at their greatest tension. Naturally he desired to go anywhere else than to the proper place, and as he reared, snorted and plunged in his fright, the old horse would look on, wondering what it was all about. Thus, many a good horse was spoiled, and each failure represented a considerable expense.

The horses of the Detroit Fire Department, 1890s. [119]

Thus, also, was the Fire Commission led to the establishment of the Department supply and training stables—the first, and, thus far, it is believed, the only institution of the kind in the country. The stables are located at the corner of Russell and Calhoun streets. The Commission obtained from the Common Council the use of that part of the old Russell street cemetery lying between Russell, Benton and Calhoun streets and the alley west of Riopelle street, a lot about 450 feet square, as a site for a truck house and these stables. Thus, also, was utilized a piece of ground that, as a dumping ground for ashes and refuse of all kinds, had been for years an unsightly blotch in the midst of a thrifty, thickly populated portion of the city.

- *1827 – Great Fire of Turku, Finland.* [184]

- *1829 – Fire destroyed hundreds of buildings in Augusta, Georgia.*
- *1831 – A fire in Fayetteville, North Carolina destroyed hundreds of buildings, and almost completely leveled the city.*
- *1835 – Second Great Fire of New York City of 1835*
- *1838 – Charleston, South Carolina, over 1,000 buildings damaged.*
- *1842 – Hamburg fire, about a quarter of the inner city destroyed, 51 killed, and an estimated 20,000 homeless.*
- *1845 – Great New York City Fire of 1845, 345 buildings destroyed*
- *1845 – Great Fire of Pittsburgh destroyed over 1,000 buildings.*
- *1845 – A fire at La Playa, the city port of Ponce, Puerto Rico, wiped out most of the Ponce vicinity in March.*
- *1846 – Great Fire of 1846 in St. John's, Newfoundland, destroyed about 2,000 buildings and left 12,000 homeless.*
- *1847 – Great Fire of Bucharest, Romania.*
- *1848 – Fire in Medina, Ohio, destroyed the entire business district.*

On the 1st of May, 1889, one year after taking possession, this area had been transformed into a park-like beauty spot, handsomely turfed, with a gracefully-designed truck house and well-built stables as accessories. The truck house is at the corner of Russell and Calhoun streets, the supply stables, built of brick, fronting on Calhoun street, and extending along the entire east side of the lot.

Supply Stables with turfed paddock, truck house and well-built stables.

A cinder track, 14 feet wide, runs around the lot, making a speeding course 700 feet long. The south or front end of the stables building is devoted to the office of the Superintendent, a dormitory for the men, storage bins and loft, harness, wagon and feed rooms, and a training room. To the rear of these are box and open stalls, where the new horses and the sick or injured horses are kept. At the extreme north end of the stables, and completely isolated from the rest, are stalls for the reception of horses ill of contagious diseases. It is in these stables that all Department horses not in actual service are quartered; here that all newly-purchased animals are so trained that when one of them takes his place in a team it is difficult to distinguish the novice from the veteran.

The training room already spoken of is practically the apparatus of an engine house in miniature. Upon the floor is a hose cart carrying 1,000 feet of hose, and at the rear of this cart are two stalls with doors, which, held by Cooper trip-levers, are operated exactly as are the stall doors in all engine houses, simultaneously with the sounding of the gong. Swinging harness is suspended from the ceiling above the pole of the hose cart.

Now comes the giving of a lesson. A veteran is placed in one of the stalls, and as he sees the plain double doors shut just ahead of him, he seems to recognize the situation, and feel his responsibility as a tutor. In the next stall is a great, handsome bay, sleek, docile and strong, but somewhat curious as to the bareness of his stall. When all is ready, the gong is sounded, the doors fly open, the equine pedagogue hurries to his place under the harness, and while men are busy snapping the collar and the quick-hitching devices, the pupil—well, it is hard to say, definitely, what a horse will do on the occasion of his first lesson. According to the disposition and intelligence of the horses the experiences vary. There have been rare instances where the

Detroit Fire department horses starting a lesson, 1912. [121]

amateur proved to be so good an imitator that he would be but two or three seconds behind his experienced model in getting into position, and who would undergo the experience of receiving the new harness in its novel and sudden appearance without a tremor. There have been experiences, also, and these are rare, where a score of lessons made no impression toward removing the excitement and fear of the pupil. Ordinarily, a new horse, after being made familiar with the fact that the sounding of the gong opens his stall doors, realizes, also, from the object lesson that trots out of the adjoining stall that he is expected to trot likewise. Then, gradually, he learns that the apparatus in front of him is harmless, that the swinging harness inflicts no injury as it is pulled down upon his back, and that the men who are engaged at various points about his anatomy are, like himself, only parts of an interesting entity. Then comes the run. Out of the doorway, in answer to the urging of the driver and to the clanging of the footboard gong, the novice goes with the old stager; the sky, the clear way ahead, the fresh air, and the efforts of his side partner, all combine to point the way, and, before he is fairly aware of the fact, the beginner is racing away with all the speed within his power, going he does not know where, and coming back he does not care when. And so, the instruction progresses. The hose is laid in his presence, men shout, the gong rings, and, so far as possible, all the real-thing accessories, such as noise and excitement, are provided for his education, until at last the horse accepts the experience in all us details as an achievement in which he is the principal participant.

- *1849 – St. Louis Fire of 1849, saw the first US firefighter killed in the line of duty.* [184]

- *1849 – First Great Fire of Toronto of 1849*
- *1850 – Kraków Fire of 1850, Poland, affects 10% of the city area. The fire made the city government increase the fire fighting budget, though the first (voluntary) fire service would not be established until 1865.* [185]

- *1851 – San Francisco Fire of 1851 destroys 2,000 buildings.*
- *1852 – Vaasa, Finland*
- *1852 – Great Montreal Fire of 1852 in Montreal left 10,000 of the city's 57,000 residents homeless.*
- *1854 – The Great fire of Newcastle and Gateshead, England, started by a spectacular explosion, killed 53 and leveled substantial property in both towns.*

"Do the horses really exhibit evidences of interest and pride in making a quick response to an alarm?" was asked of an old driver. "Do they! Well, I should say yes! Nothing so disgusts a horse as delay, after he has done his duty in getting under a harness. Sometimes a snap will bother us, the collar will not come together, or a strap is obstinate, and—maybe you don't believe it, but I've seen horses look around with an expression on their face, plainly saying, 'Oh, hurry up there!' Then, when they feel the bit tighten, see them settle for the haul, and off they go, slowly and restrained at first, to at last settle down to a steady and by no means slow gallop."

Exercising horses attached to a skeleton wagon. Handwriting on the back: "Detroit Fire Department approx. 1902. Engine 9 exercise wagon shown with the steamer horses. If a fire company had no runs within a 24 hour period, the horses were exercised in local streets near the station houses. In the event of a fire, they would be notified to return to the station by ringing the tower bell." [120]

In the old days, it was a common thing at all of the engine houses to give exhibition hitches for the entertainment of visitors, but that practice has been abolished, and well it is so, because the courtesy was valueless to both visitors and horses and to the firemen. The horses quickly recognized an exhibition call, and would mope disconsolately out from their stalls, or else refuse point blank to be shown off. Under present regulations, horses are trained not only to go to the pole, but to be hitched and go out of the house when the gong strikes. No horse is run out unless he is to be exercised or to go to a fire.

Every team in the Department is exercised at stated times each secular day for a period of ninety minutes, unless the weather is bad, or the company has had a long run a few hours preceding the regular time for exercising. The horses are attached to a skeleton wagon and jogged at a rate of speed not exceeding five miles an hour. No driver is permitted to go more than three squares away from quarters, and in case of an alarm the team is summoned by means of a few taps on the bell in quick succession. When exercising, the horses wear the regular harness, so that all that is necessary upon their being called in for a run is to shift the team from the exercise wagon to the engine, truck or wagon.

When a horse is purchased, a record is made of the transaction in the "Horse Book." The age, color, weight, sex, and purchase price, as well as the name and residence of the seller, are noted. The horse is given a number, which he retains as long as he remains in the service. If he dies, the certificate of the veterinary officer appears on the record. If he is sold, a certificate of the date and cause of sale and length of time in service is recorded. The amount received is converted into the city treasury as the proceeds of the sale of a horse, stating the number, thus completing the record of each individual animal. As a new horse comes in, he receives a tag reading like this: "D. F. D., 250," signifying that he is horse No. 250. This tag is fastened to the halter and goes with the horse from place to place. In the Commissioners' office a large board contains cards showing the location of different horses, these cards being changed whenever the horses are moved. Four years represents the life of the average Fire Department horse, although there are now a number of horses who have been much longer in service. (photos courtesy of Detroit Historical Society, DFD Legacy and http://www.detroit.fdmaps.com/)

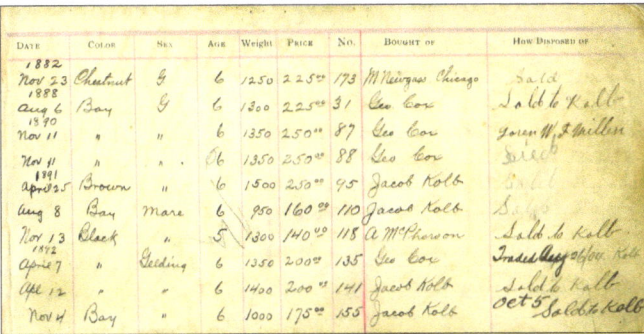

One of Martin Coney's legers held by the Detroit Historical Society. [122]

Auction Day at the great horse market, Detroit, Mich. [123]

- *1858 – A large fire in Auckland, New Zealand, destroyed 3 hotels, 20 shops, more than 50 houses, the police station, theater, post office and several other buildings in the centre of town, an entire city block. At the time Auckland had a population of about 6,300.*
- *1862 – Troy, New York, 671 buildings destroyed*
- *1864 – Great Fire of Brisbane in Queensland, Australia, burned over four city blocks with over 50 houses and dozens of businesses razed*
- *1861–1865 – The American Civil War involved several major city fires:*
- *1861 – Charleston, South Carolina*
- *1864 – Atlanta, Georgia, burned after time given for evacuation of citizens by order of William Tecumseh Sherman*
- *1865 – Columbia, South Carolina, burned while being occupied by troops commanded by William Tecumseh Sherman*
- *1865 – Richmond, Virginia, burned by retreating Confederates.*
- *1866 – Great Portland Fire of 1866, Maine, destroyed the commercial district and left 10,000 homeless.* [186]

Fire Horse Stories

One might say the most romantic and regal era of firefighting was when horses were the true horsepower of the engines and trucks. The heartwarming stories of the animals' loyalty, bravery and commitment are the stuff of urban legend.

Mack served the Rescue firemen faithfully in York, Pennsylvania for 25 years. [124]

OLD MACK

For 25 years Mack served the Rescue firemen faithfully in York, Pennsylvania. For a large part of that time being their only hose apparatus horse. A powerful bay, he dragged the apparatus at a speed which brought exclamations of, "Look out for Mack," whenever the alarm sounded. On one occasion he nobly responded to a command to take the apparatus through a narrow passageway in the south end between flaming walls. He came out with all the hair burned from one side of his body. Mack knew the difference between the test alarms and real fire alarms, his dash from his stall to his place at the apparatus being much more vigorous on the latter occasions. In one instance when the sounding of an alarm at night found the lights in the engine house all extinguished, Mack was impatiently waiting in his place when they were resumed. His unfailing instinct had enabled him to go there directly in the dark. After Mack's retirement, the firemen realized that if taken from the engine house he would soon pine away and die. Accordingly, he was given a box stall at the rear of the stalls of the horses in active service. He made a number of appearances in public, chiefly in firemen's parades. The firefighters of the Rescue felt that Mack's loyalty and longevity deserved special recognition. Well before his death, they established a fund to provide for a respectful burial plot and monument. In 1913, a 5-foot tall granite monument was placed over his grave, inscribed with, "In memory of Mack, the noble horse of the Rescue Fire Company of York, Pa. Died Dec. 3, 1911. Aged 32 years." The monument features a full-size relief of Mack's head, carved on the granite. After the York County Fire Museum was established the monument was moved to the yard beside the museum. Mack's remains were re-interred next to the monument, however not before Mack made a final fire call. While his remains were being transferred to the Fire Museum, the fireman transporting them responded to a fire call. (cited from: http://www.yorkblog.com/yorkspast/2015/12/29/exploits-mack/)

A five-foot-tall tombstone, complete with a chiseled horse's head, marks the grave of "noble horse" Mack, who died in 1911. At first he was buried in the woods, but he was later dug up, and he and his tombstone were moved next to the county fire museum. [125]

JACK AND JACK

Jack and Jack were a famous fire horse team for the Des Moines Fire Department. Old Jack was 23 at the time of his retirement. He had come to the fire department at six years old with the reputation as a "man killer." However, this was an undeserved nickname. Jack had spooked and kicked the head of his original owner, who had fallen over the dashboard of his wagon and right beneath Jack's hooves. Young Jack, who was being used as a carriage horse, was purchased for $175 by the fire department. The two became such a great team that they won a race in the 1903 Iowa State Firemen's Tournament and many thereafter, earning them the title of "World Champions." As an example of how extremely dangerous the profession was at the time, Jack and Jack collided with a streetcar while rushing to a fire, which resulted in the deaths of two firefighters. The two horses miraculously remained unscathed. Upon their retirement from the department, a councilman noted, "Usually worn out horses are turned over to the Street Department, but if I were to attempt to do that with Jack and Jack, the Fire Department would mob me." Jack and Jack spent the rest of their lives in farm pastures belonging to a firefighter's brother. (cited from: http://www.equitrekking.com/articles/entry/famous_horses_in_history_-_the_fire_horse/)

Jack and Jack were part of the first fire company "Hook & Ladder" in the City of Des Moines in 1865. [126]

FIRE HORSE FRED

Fire Horse Fred pulled the New Bern fire hose wagon from 1908 to 1925. He died in the harness pulling the crew to a false alarm. [127]

Fire Horse Fred of New Bern, North Carolina, served for 17 years pulling the company's hose wagon. He was known throughout the area as a champion hose wagon racer. He pulled at top speed while a firefighter stood on the ground, grabbed the end of the unraveling hose, screwed on the nozzle, and got the water flowing. Fred was also present during a notorious town fire that dynamited 100 homes. He helped create a firebreak and save the rest of the town. The New Bern Firemen's Museum memorializes all of the city's fire horses. Fred was so beloved that the firefighters had his head stuffed and mounted when he died at age 25, which is displayed at the New Bern Firemen's Museum (cited from: http://www.equitrekking.com/articles/entry/famous_horses_in_history_-_the_fire_horse/)

MIN AND MAC

As testimony to the ability of the fire horses to know their jobs, two horses, Min and Mac, jumped to position at the alarm but a rookie failed to connect their reins to the bit. Despite no driver control and crowded lunch hour streets, they safely navigated traffic and found the fire themselves – much to the relief of the driver.

FLORA/MAGGIE

In The Detroit Fire Department "Flora" was the name of horse No.117. In 1880, she was transferred to No.1 engine house, she acquired the name of Maggie, and in honor of her veteran driver, she became known as Maggie Scott. On one occasion, while Scott was at dinner, an alarm came in from box 6, and somehow the boys forgot about the hose carriage and Maggie, so she was not hitched. However, when the engine pulled out Maggie followed it, and she would not be stopped until the engine took its position at the hydrant. Then the old mare was contented to be caught and was led peacefully back to the engine house.

The fire horses were "members of the family"

The Detroit Fire Department

- *1868 – Auerbach in der Oberpfalz, Bavaria. Arson destroyed 107 houses and 146 other buildings; 4 deaths.*
- *1869 – Great Fire of Whitstable of 1869, Kent, England, fed by strong winds, destroying 71 buildings.*
- *1870 – Fire in Medina, Ohio, started in a wooden building with a barber shop and consumed all but two blocks of the business district, nearly wiping out the entire town.*
- *1871 – Fires deliberately set during the Paris Commune in May destroyed the Royal Palace of the Tuileries, the Louvre Library, the Palais de Justice, the Hôtel de Ville, the Gare de Lyon, and the Palais d'Orsay.*
- *1871 – Strong winds fed several simultaneous fires in Wisconsin, Michigan and Illinois on Oct. 8–9:*
- *1871 – Great Chicago Fire of 1871 destroyed the downtown on October 8 and died out the following night. About 250 dead.* [187]

- *1871 – Peshtigo Fire of 1871, several towns destroyed in a firestorm that reached Michigan, 1,500–2,500 dead. Deadliest wildfire in American history.*
- *1871 – Great Michigan Fire of 1871 was a series of simultaneous fires, the most prominent of which was the Port Huron Fire, which killed over 200 people in Port Huron, MI.*

CHUBBY

Chubby was the last Rochester, New York, fire horse. He retired in 1926. A stunning white Percheron, he was the town favorite and struck many a pose. Due to his longevity and striking appearance, Chubby was the best-known of the city fire horses, with Fire Chief Maurice Keating calling him "one of the strongest, most willing and good-natured ever in the fire department."

(cited from: http://www.craftcompany.com/firefighter.html)

Chubby with fireman Frank Kalb. [128]

BILL

In the little city of Watertown, New York, Bill was a member of its first fire team. He grew up with the department,

Bill and Chubby - Engine Company No. 6, Rochester, NY. Craft Company No. 6. [130]

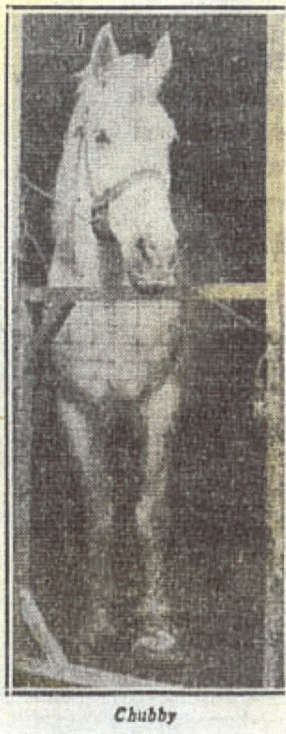

February 21, 1933
Obituary for the popular retired fire horse Chubby. [129]

attaining such perfection that he could be transferred to any of the five companies in the town, shown his place, whether in double or three horse hitch, put in his stall, and when the bell rang he would be first to dash out, invariably to the post assigned him. If a less perfect associate usurped the place he was to occupy, he would attack the unfortunate with ferocity, biting and shoving until he drove the other from his station. He seemed born to the service, heart and soul he was a fire horse, and could he have chosen undoubtedly, he would have selected the end that came to him, for he dropped dead in harness, while drawing a hose wagon back from an alarm. (cited from: http://www.mi-harness.net/publct/tpr/firehorse.html)

DAN

Dan, also of the Watertown, New York Fire Department, was a blue-blooded Hackney that in his youth had won a blue ribbon at the National Horse Show in Madison Square Garden. Purchased by an upstate fancier, he was sold to the city after exhibiting a tendency to run away. The fire chief, who took him as his driver, found Dan amenable to spoken orders and the horse thus handled, proved gentle and tractable. He did duty thirteen years when retired to farm life and lived to a ripe twenty-six. (cited from: http://www.mi-harness.net/publct/tpr/firehorse.html)

GEORGE HALE'S TEAM

The world's most famous fire team was trained by Fire Chief George Hale of Kansas City. Hale toured Europe with them and 17 chosen firemen, demonstrating American fire-fighting methods. For their trip to Paris, firefighters took horses Buck, Mack and Charlie. The animals became familiar to thousands of Kansas City residents who watched them drill almost daily in preparation for the trip. Later thousands of people saw his horses at the St. Louis Exposition in 1904, where he was chief of the exposition department and his world champion team drew a hose wagon. Running to a fire the pair kept stride; every movement was uniform. They demonstrated almost human intelligence. The wagon was placed in the street, the harness swung upon a frame over the pole, and the horses were removed a block away behind the rig. A gong was sounded and instantly the chargers wheeled about and dashed to their place, fifty yards away. Years later, when Hale had retired and the Kansas City department had been motorized, one of these-horses was brought in from the country where he was passing his old age, for he was 32. For 11 years he had not heard the station gong. The old disused wagon was brought out and its harness attached. The bell sounded an imaginary alarm. The horse was standing placidly some distance away, but at the sound the years seemed to pass from him and there was no faltering -as he galloped to the shafts and backed under the harness. (cited from: http://www.mi-harness.net/publct/tpr/firehorse.html)

Famous fire team trained by Fire Chief George Hale of Kansas City. [132]

Kansas city fire horses drilling in preparation for their trip to Paris. [131]

HORSES OF THE FIRE DEPARTMENT OF NEW YORK

In the early 1900's Chief Edward Croker of the Fire Department of New York (FDNY) and his driver John Rush, along with a horse named Bullet, were often seen "Whirling over icy streets, skidding on wet pavements, many times wheels were smashed and the chief and his driver missed death or injury by inches."– The New York Sun, April 26, 1912 By this time chiefs in the FDNY were using automobiles to respond to fires, but a few horse-drawn buggies were kept in reserve because motorized vehicles were not always reliable. As the personal chauffeur for New York Fire Department Chief Edward Croker in the early 1900s, John Rush's nickname was Dare-Devil Rush. Fellow firemen often made bets that Chief Croker's wild horse, Bullet, would determine the fate of John Rush. In later years, only a few believed that he would survive while driving Croker's high-power automobile 50 miles an hour through the city's congested streets. John Rush eventually became Battalion Chief. No one ever dreamed that Battalion Chief Rush would be killed in an accident while being driven leisurely home for lunch in a buggy harnessed to Victor, the horse of Engine Company No. 30. (cited from: http://hatchingcatnyc.com/2015/06/10/1912-victor-the-new-york-fire-horse-that-finally-lost-it-on-varick-street/)

Chief Edward Croker in white hat with horse Bullet. By this time chiefs in the FDNY were using automobiles to respond to fires, but a few horse-drawn buggies were kept in reserve because motorized vehicles were not always reliable. [133]

Chief Edward Croker and his driver in Croker's 1901 steam-driven buggy, the Locomobile. [134]

The archives of the New York Fire Department tell stories of many horses! In the early eighties there was a horse with Engine Company No. 9 in North Moore street that would back from his stall when thirsty, go to the water tap, turn on the water and after drinking, turn off the faucet and return to his stall. At 23 Alameda had mastered the business so thoroughly in his 16 years at fire houses that when his harness was lowered to the floor he would hoist it with his teeth and swing it upon himself. In April, 1910, his name appeared in a list of 100 steeds condemned and to be sold at auction, but protests grew so imperative that he was transferred to a fuel wagon and retained. Engine 17 had a horse that the men believed could count. He appeared to know the box alarms to which his company responded and showed it by dashing to his place. When other calls came he would pull the dormitory gong, thus turning the men out of their beds. When they came sliding down the pole he would indicate his pleasure by neighing. He not only would leave his stall to drink but would fill a pail and carry it to his mate. A majority of fire horses were rendered temporarily deaf while participating in a July Fourth parade in 1909. They suffered paralysis of the auditory nerve through the concussion of firecrackers and guns fired in the celebration. At the next alarm a number of the animals failed to take their places and showed no haste when the drivers urged them, but as soon as their hearing was restored they resumed their duty as efficiently as before (cited from: http://www.mi-harness.net/publct/tpr/firehorse.html)

SKIDOO

Often firefighters would be interviewed by local newspapers about their "celebrity" horses. This account appeared in the Los Angeles Record on July 11, 1906. "My old nag Skidoo is the best on earth, bar none," says Fire Chief Lips. "He is about 17 years old and has been with the department nine years. He was bought by Ed Smith when he was assistant chef, and only cost about $8. Skidoo is a genius in the horse line. He makes up to nobody, and about 6 months ago nearly bit a couple of fingers off the hand of one of the street sprinkling inspectors who was trying to pet him. I can call 'whoa' to Skidoo, jump out of the wagon, and be gone half a day, and when I go back he will be right where I left him. He will stand for hours and not move an inch. The old horse is blind in one eye, but that doesn't detract from his worth. He has never drawn an engine, for he is too small and light for that work, but he is a dandy in the chief's wagon. Last year he was all run down, and I put him in pasture for about 6 weeks. He was with 8 or 9 other fire horses but he would have nothing to do with them. He would stand by himself for hours. Perhaps he thought that he should maintain that chief's dignity. Skidoo is still a goer despite his advanced years, and his wind is good. He will go anywhere and everywhere, and about as fast as you would care to ride."
(cited from: http://www.lafire.com/stations/archive/articles/fs003_1906-0711_1906newspaperbook_FireChiefPrefersSkidoo.htm)

HORSES OF THE RICHMOND, INDIANA FIRE DEPARTMENT
DEPENDABLE DICK

The last horse drafted into service by the Richmond, Indiana Fire Department was Dependable Dick, who was purchased when he was 6 years old. Dick served in the hook and ladder company with Old Joe, a veteran horse with whom Dick could get along, as Dick needed mentoring. Trouble was the youngster couldn't get used to the starting of the truck with the doors closed. When the horses heard the bell, they were supposed to light out, but Dick lagged until Old Joe yanked the wheels far enough to trip the door release. It was then Dick would then throw in and surge forth and do his bit and pull. One day the driver decided to break Dick of this habit and slapped him with a whip. Unused to such treatment, Dick tore out full bore, the harness rings snapped and his head crashed through glass in the door. Several stitches had to be taken to close the resulting wound. We decided to let Dick be after that. Being dependable for breakneck speed was how Dependable Dick got his name.

Richmond Fire Department hose House No. 1 horses and firemen from early in the 20th century. [135]

Proud steeds and crew at Richmond Fire Dept. Hose House No. 4. [136]

BOB

Another horse, Bob, was purchased for the fire Chief's buggy, but Bob proved too skittish. On one fire run he charged out Central Station in panic and landed in an open stairway leading to a basement on Fifth and Main, with the buggy on top of him. He was also very hard to handle. Later upon being sent to the West Side Fire Station, Bob got paired with Old Joe, the horse that tutored Dick. It was here Bob blossomed and the team became noted for speed, and the department couldn't have too many runs in a day to suit them. One reason was both horses liked tobacco. They would get a chaw and it sort of started a fire in them. Bob would follow members of the department around like a big dog begging for a clump of sugar or 'bacca. He would make noises until crew members gathered around. The minute they went to bed he would start again. Whenever the vet was called, the horse was pronounced fine. That, however, did not relieve the fire crew from sitting up nights because the horse decided he was lonesome and wanted company.

RODNEY

Rodney was a horse that would run his heart out as far as North 10th and E, but there was a magical line he would stop at and lay down in harness, panting. He went only so far and no further. Rodney lasted a short time.

HORSES OF WORLD WAR I

Two Richmond fire horses laid down their lives for the country. In World War I, Bob and King were drafted into the Army and sent overseas. They perished on the battlefield, and it was a grievance to the fire department. (cited from: https://www.pal-item.com/story/news/local/2017/06/18/out-our-past-fire-department-used-rely-4-legged-heroes/405104001/)

- *1871 – The Urbana fire destroyed central Urbana, Illinois, on October 9.*
- *1872 – Great Boston Fire of 1872, destroyed 776 buildings and killed at least 20 people.* [188]

- *1874 – Chicago Fire of 1874, July 14, was in some respects very similar to the 1871 fire, but was stopped by a new fire-proof wall. It destroyed 812 structures and killed 20 people.*
- *1875 – Great Whiskey Fire, Dublin, 18 June, killed 13 people, and destroyed a malt house, a bonded warehouse, houses and a tannery in Mill Street and Chamber Street.*
- *1877 – Paris, Texas, the first of three fires that destroyed much of the town.*
- *1877 – Saint John, New Brunswick, fire destroyed 1,600 buildings.*
- *1878 – The Great Fire of Hong Kong destroyed 350 to 400 buildings across more than 10 acres (40,000 m2) of central Hong Kong.*
- *1879 – Hakodate fire, Hakodate, Hokkaidō, Japan, caused 67 fatalities, 20,000 homeless.*
- *1880 – On 25 September, another fire took place destroying most of the older civil records (births, baptisms, marriages, etc.) of the Ponce, Puerto Rico, parish.*

HORSE NO. 12 - WASHINGTON DC

In the early morning hours of March 30, 1890, in Washington, D.C., the collision of two horse-drawn fire wagons racing to answer an alarm seemed a minor matter. The vehicles—a hose cart and a heavy steam engine—continued on their way to the fire. As they raced across town, the driver of the hose cart noticed that one of his two-horse team, Horse No. 12, limped somewhat. When they arrived at the scene of the alarm, the horse pulled up lame. The driver made a shocking discovery. The animal had lost its left rear foot, apparently run over and cut off in the collision with the heavy engine. The horse had galloped to the fire—nearly a mile—on its stump. Through the tears of attending fire fighters and policemen, it was quickly put down with a shot. No one had ever known such an animal as Horse No. 12—conditioned by the chaos of the city's emergencies that in this instance was his last. In an era in which horses and horse-drawn vehicles predominated in daily life, the newspapers noted that the "equine hero" had "performed a service that was perhaps never before equaled." The story went viral. Such was the outpouring of affection for the horse that one reader in Indiana suggested that the city's authorities might have saved it with a bandage and retired it to pasture. Cauterized and preserved with a coat of shiny black enamel, the hoof of Horse No. 12 lived on as a memorial in the District of Columbia Fire Department. The Smithsonian exhibited the hoof as a loan, and later accepted it as a gift through the department's chief engineer, R. W. Dutton. Its placement in the National Museum, Dutton hoped, would "perpetuate the memory of an animal whose bravery and devotion to duty placed him high upon the department roll of honor." (cited from: http://americanhistory.si.edu/blog/hoof-fire-horse-number-12)

Cauterized and preserved hoof of Horse No. 12. District of Columbia Fire Department. [137]

- *1881 – Thumb Fire in Michigan burned over a million acres during a drought, 282 killed.*
- *1883 – In mid August, a Great Fire broke out in Kuala Terengganu, Terengganu, destroying the royal palace and 1,600 buildings, many housing gunpowder.*
- *1886 – Fire in Calgary, Alberta* [189]

- *1886 – Great Vancouver Fire, Vancouver, British Columbia*
- *1888 – Sundsvall Fire of 1888, Sweden, left 9,000 homeless.*
- *1889 – Great Seattle Fire, Washington, destroyed the central business district* [190]

- *1889 – Great Spokane Fire, Washington, destroyed the downtown commercial district.*
- *1889 – Great Ellensburg Fire, Washington, resulted in the city's bid to become the state capital ending in failure.*
- *1889 – Great Bakersfield Fire of 1889, California, destroyed 196 buildings and killed 1 person.*

HORSES OF THE PORTLAND, OREGON FIRE DEPARTMENT

COLONEL

Colonel, a white gelding was 21 years when in service in 1904. He would become so excited at the sound of the gong that twice he left the engine house before his driver was ready. Following the lead steamer, Colonel would pull his hose cart to the box, find the nearest hydrant, and wait to be hitched.

JERRY

Jerry, was a big horse with 21 years in service in 1911. He was Portland's most heralded fire horse. He was so smart that men swear he winked when he heard them making favorable comments about him. He served long and well and became best known for gallantry as he snatched a hat off his handler, tipping it if a lady was passing.

BLIND DICK

Blind Dick was so loyal to the fire service that he hauled the supply wagon when he grew too old to run with a steamer (cited from: https://www.portlandoregon.gov/fire/article/384861)

The Kenton Firehouse, dedicated in 1913, was the first city-built station in North Portland. The facility, with its distinctive Second Renaissance Revival architecture, was built on land donated by a subsidiary of the Swift Meat Company. [138]

Fire Station 2, at 510 NW Third Avenue, was in service from 1912 to 1950, fire station near Northwest 3rd Avenue and Glisan. Portland, OR. [139]

JIM

Jim, the most handsome, strongest, best trained, and most responsive, dependable horse on the department, was Toledo's most distinguished specimen of equine intelligence and fidelity; and, he was the unending pride of Engine House No. 3. Such an ideal fire horse he was, that he was in the process of having his portrait painted by the artist, H.C.N Crandall, for exposition on the wall at the Museum of Art. It was the exemplary Jim who always responded first to alarms and ran with unerring accuracy, in his lead position of the 3-horse hitch on the large steamer at headquarters. It was after such an alert response to the 9th alarm of the day, that his driver, Charles Harrison, clasping the heavy harness about Jim's massive neck, observed the horse was standing unflinchingly at his post of duty upon three legs, and that his left hind leg hung helplessly from his body. Hurried examination proved the valuable animal's leg was broken and he was taken from his central place in the engine trio forever. Toledo's finest veterinary surgeons were called, but it was declared that the horse could not be saved and he was put-down by a new modern method of injecting positive poison in the jugular vein. When and how Jim's leg was broken is a mystery. He had responded to 8 calls during the day and was willing to respond to the 9th. The horse was only 7 ½ years old and had only served the fire department for 2 years, but in that short time had proved himself to be the finest and most accurately trained. He also had the honor of being the most perfect specimen of equine beauty and symmetry of the city's lot of exceptional horses. He was a very large dapple gray, beautifully marked. (cited from: https://www.merrimacknh.gov/about-fire-rescue/pages/horses-in-fire-service)

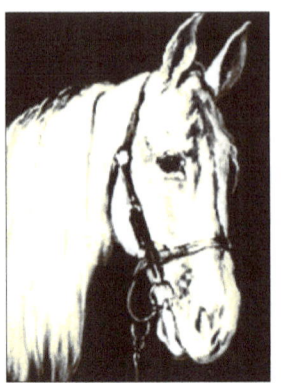

Jim's portrait painted by the artist, H.C.N Crandall. - After 25 years of searching, Mike Tressler, writer for the Toledo Blade and Toledo Fire Department historian, Bill O'Connor, have located the famous painting of Jim the Fire Horse. "We received an e-mail recently from Mrs. Molly Cowan, Sylvania, OH, who inherited the portrait from her mother." The painting has been in her family for many years, originally having belonged to her grandfather, Harry J. Smith. Jim's portrait has lovingly hung in Mrs. Cowan's home and someday may eventually find itself at home in the museum in the special stall reserved for him. [141]

Some firemen risked charges for slow responses in order to prevent a horse from being deemed unfit for service. Horse's retirements were announced in the paper. Most retired horses went to live in a pasture in the country and some were sold to locals as delivery horses. Often funerals were held for fire horse heroes.

Funeral procession for a fire horse. [142]

ONCE A FIRE HORSE ALWAYS A FIRE HORSE

Horses were very aware of what the gong meant – even sometimes when they were no longer serving as fire horses. A former New York fire charger employed by a refuse collector, calling for rubbish at an engine house, galloped out when the gong sounded, wrecking the station stairs and doing other damage.

A Williamsburg milkman perhaps was unaware his old horse had been a member of the department until one day an engine passed as he was delivering milk on the Bowery. Instantly the animal took the bit in his teeth and made off behind the steamer, while milk cans bumped out of the reeling wagon.

At Utica, New York, in November, 1908, the team of No. 9 engine was being given its morning exercise when they chanced to meet another company responding to an alarm. No. 9's team nearly got away from the driver in an endeavor to follow the apparatus.

Tom had served so ably that the city of New York granted him a pension, stipulating that he be kept

Old Joe, The Veteran Fire Horse
Artist, Herbert Johnson, 1922. [143]

in his own station. Tom was tied in his stall, but at the first alarm he nearly wrecked it in his efforts to respond. So vigorously did he kick and pull that the men abandoned this method, believing that after he had been refused his place he would not trouble them. They did not know Tom. As long as he remained he would hurry to his harness each time the summons came, and when led aside he would return slowly and voluntarily to his stall. (cited from: http://www.mi-harness.net/publct/tpr/firehorse.html)

"Our Fire Horses
 GLORIOUS
 In beauty and in service;
 Faithful Friends
 We cannot call them dumb
 Because they spoke in deeds
 In every hour of danger
 Perpetual remembrance
 Enshrines their loyalty and courage"

TRUE PALS

The Rochester American Legion created a bronze plaque in 1926 that fittingly describes all fire horses. [144]

The following is an excerpt from the memoirs of a fireman in Los Angeles, 1909:

The fire horses were most human and very smart; to cite one instance, one fireman at Engine 4 walked in his sleep, fell down the pole hole, and lay there in front of the horse's stall, near fatally injured. That horse knew something was wrong so he began to kick on the side of the stall which awakened members who slid the pole and found the man with a fractured skull. He would have died but for this act of the fire horse. Then another time the horses were hitched by some of the firemen on the engine and then they got on the apparatus; the driver did not for some reason get on the driver's seat. Those fire horses followed the hose wagon out of the station onto Aliso Street to Fourth and Main Street with no driver. The Engineer on the rear of the Engine saw no driver on the seat and climbed over the hose suctions with the Engine swaying from side to side, reached the seat of the apparatus and drove the horses to the fire. No one of today can know how these human-like lovable fire horses were loved by the boys at the fire stations and the public. These fire horses always giving their best, running at full speed down the streets, and in hot weather foam sweat upon their bodies. Sometimes falling and getting hurt but never quitting; always loyal to duty. Some say that when fire horses passed out of history so went life out of the history of the pioneers' most loved animals. these pioneers and fire horses were the start of the great fire department of today. But, no one can take out of our memory the true pals, the fire horses; we loved them and they loved us. (courtesy of LAFD Historical Society)

- 1889 – The First Great Fire of Lynn, Massachusetts, destroyed about 100 buildings and took over 2 weeks to put out.
- 1892 – Great Fire of 1892 in St. John's, Newfoundland [191]

- 1893 – Clarksville, Virginia, fire destroyed many of the blocks between the river (now the Kerr Reservoir) and 5th Street in the historic commercial core.
- 1894 – Great Hinckley Fire, Minnesota was a firestorm that destroyed several towns; over 400 killed.
- 1894 – Great Fire in Shanghai destroyed over 1,000 buildings.
- 1896 – Paris, Texas, the second of three fires that destroyed much of the town.
- 1897 – The Great Fire of Windsor, Nova Scotia, Canada, destroyed 80% of the town.
- 1898 – Great Fire of New Westminster, British Columbia
- 1898 – Great fire of Park City, Utah
- 1899 – El Polvorin Fire in Ponce, Puerto Rico, occurred on January 25. The fire started at the U.S. Munitions Depot (on the lot currently occupied by the Ponce High School). The heroes in that fire are remembered with monuments and an obelisk in Plaza Las Delicias.

The Public Relations Team of the Fire Department

There is no doubt that the fire horses were heroes in their cities and towns. Fire Departments often had children visit the horses to offer them treats – and of course pose for pictures. Newspapers often ran stories about the horses at the fire houses. Framed photographs of favorites horses hung on firehouse walls, and citizens knew many of them by name. Tom and Harry were a pair of 1,800-pound brutes who were the stars of the Detroit Fire Department Ladder 1. "When Ladder No. 1 was called to a downtown fire, hundreds stopped to admire the horses," recalled one old Detroiter. "Tom and Harry were the recipients of a lot of candy from women in the shopping district." (cited from: http://www.dfdlegacy.com/detroit-fire-department-history-last-running-of-the-fire-horses/)

Many fire departments also taught the horses tricks to amuse their visitors. Frank and Dan were 2 horses owned by the Durham, North Carolina Fire Department. To handle these fine horses, William Herzo Teer (nicknamed Soky) was hired. He was probably the best horse rider ever seen, outside of a circus. 'Soky' used to tie Dan and Frank's heads together, stand spaddle legged upon their backs, and ride Roman style up and down Holloway Street, until the Chief made him stop. (cited from: https://legeros.com/history/horses/various.shtml)

Los Angeles Fire Department, Lt. Loebel with neighbor boy back of Engine House 12. [145]

Young boy Frankie Williams with "Dimple," fire department horse, Seattle, 1922. The Seattle Fire Department held a parade down 2nd Avenue in November 1922 as part of a farewell to veteran horses like "Dimple," shown here with a little boy outside Station 35. In June 1924, it was announced in the Seattle Times that all fire horses would be retired. [146]

If the fire horses were racing down the street, there were always spectators on the curb watching them fly by. Children would run behind or follow on bikes. Many a child came home late at night after a day of watching the gallant fire horses.

Los Angeles fire engine on a hard pull up First St. Hill, 1900. [148]

The Cleveland Fire Department's Engine NO. 2, 1910. [147]

Children running along with the Ladder Truck as it speeds to a fire.

When the fire horses were posing for a picture, there were curious children – and adults too – ready to be in the pictures with the celebrated horses.

Horses were heroes and changed the viewpoint of people that horses were just "mindless machines"; they were well respected, intelligent comrades.

Fire horses have inspired children's books too. "Rookie Fireman" is a book written by Sioux City native Margaret Crary. It is the story of Paddy and Prince, the celebrated fire horse team of the early 1900's. She dedicated the book to retired firefighter Theodore McElhouse who knew the horses. The horses were acclaimed as world champions in the bunk hitch race. In the story, the gallant fire horses are leaving to make way for motorized fire engines, and a young man goes to extreme lengths to give his favorite horse the best possible retirement.

Just as fire engines are popular in parades today, so were the horses and apparatus in the parades of the early 1900's.

On Sept. 1, 1898, Bowling Green, KY's first paid fire department came into existence. [149]

Paddy and Prince [151]

Fourth of July early 1900's--Horse-Drawn Fire Wagon #1 is decorated for the parade. According to the caption embedded at the top of the photo, "the following year, the Victor Fire Department won the World Hose Run Championship in San Francisco." [152]

Bowling Green Fire Department Horse and Buggy Parade. [150]

So popular were fire fighters and their horses that there was an exhibit at the 1904 St. Louis World's Fair featuring firefighting. The attraction was operated by George Hale, legendary Kansas City Fire Chief, who ascended into celebrity status while receiving first prize at the 1893 International Fire Tournament in London. The building at the Fair contained a 5,000-seat auditorium to house the 50-minute show. Hale repeated the extravaganza 4 times daily. The show began with information on how the fire wagons worked as well as draft horses leaping through `fire.' The set switched to a New York City street and illustrated how the brave firefighters were alerted, responded and dealt with a 6 story building fire. There were women and children to be rescued, while hoses fought the `blaze,' the strongest men pumped the `water.'

The interesting fact for this attraction was that there was no fire used in this spectacle. Special effects and stage tricks which included: steam, electricity, film, stained glass, silk, celluloid and assorted mechanics and physical effects created a realistic illusion of a building on fire. At the end, the building collapsed after the rescue of its inhabitants. After the show, the crowd gazed at a collection of old and new firefighting equipment. New York sent 2 fire wagons once pumped by George Washington and Benedict Arnold. There was a 2,000-seat restaurant in the exhibit as well. (cited from: http://atthefair.homestead.com/pkeatt/Halesfirefighter.html)

Hale's Firefighters, 1893. [153]

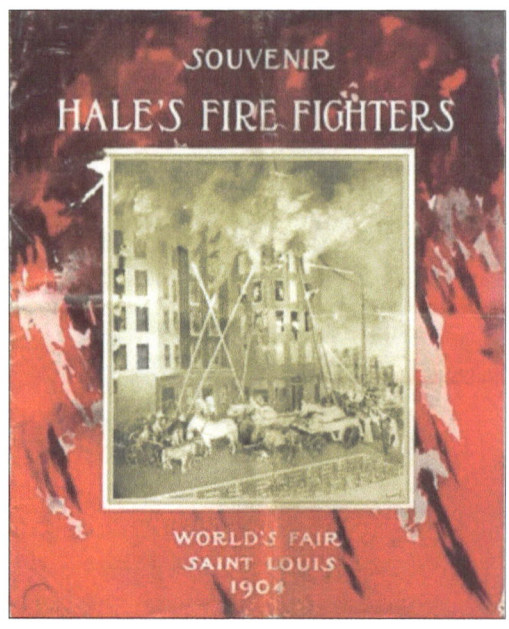

Souvenir, Hale's Fire Fighters, World's Fair Saint Louis, 1904. [155]

Hale's Firefighters celebrated Pompier Life-saving Corps. The members of this corps are Captain Al Graefer, Adolph Graefer, Henry Schaffnit, Irs Jackson, Frederick Wilson, William McCornwell, George Phipps and Sylvester Ingram. [154]

People knew the names of the horses in their local fire departments. The horses were well loved and mourned when injured.

Joe and Dan were the celebrated horses of George Hale of Kansas City who went to Europe and astonished the world with their amazing time of hitching in less than 15 seconds. Fire horses Dan and Joe were snow-white Arabian horses, known through the city as top-notch fire horses. Joe was killed in the line of duty in 1894 in a horrible fire engine-cable car collision. His partner, Dan, however, was retired to Swope Park in 1907 and died of old age in 1913. It is said that long after his duty days were past him, Dan would still come running at the sound of a bell.

In her book, My Revelation, Loula Long Combs recalls, "About a month after the team returned from London (and you may be sure it was a warm welcome that greeted them on their arrival), Joe and Dan were back on duty; the alarm had sounded and they were on their way to a fire. At Eleventh and Broadway, they collided with a streetcar, and Joe received a severe leg injury. Everything was done to save the gallant animal. You can imagine how concerned everyone felt about the injury and suffering of one of this wonder team. Men, women, and children called at the Fire Department headquarters to inquire about Joe and to leave sugar, apples, and carrots. In spite of all the loving care, Joe died; and I am sure many a tear was shed for the brave horse that gave his life in line of duty." (cited from: https://archive.org/stream/myrevelation027243mbp/myrevelation027243mbp_djvu.txt)

Joe and Dan, the celebrated horses of George Hale of Kansas City, Missouri. This photo shows a horse-drawn fire wagon running on Westport Road near Pennsylvania Avenue in preparation for the fire department's trip to Paris in 1900. Having competed in the International Fire Congress competition in England in 1893, they won the Gold Medal for their innovative firefighting abilities under the command of long-time Fire Chief George Hale. The team, along with fire horses "Dan" and "Joe," also won first place awards in the hitching competition – reaching the scene and throwing water all in an elapsed time of 8.5 sec. [156]

- *1900 – Hull–Ottawa Fire of 1900, Canada. Starting in Hull, Quebec, the fire crossed the river to Ottawa, Ontario, and destroyed large areas of both cities.*
- *1900 – Sandon, British Columbia, Canada, destroyed by fire.*
- *1901 – Great Jacksonville Fire of 1901 in Jacksonville, Florida, destroyed the downtown area with flames seen for hundreds of miles.*
- *1902 – The Great Conflagration, Paterson, New Jersey*
- *1904 – Great Baltimore Fire of 1904*
- *1904 – Second Great Fire of Toronto of 1904*
- *1904 – Yazoo City, Mississippi (USA) fire, 25 May, destroyed entire business district of ca. 125 buildings; US$2,000,000 in damages.*
- *1904 – Ålesund Fire, 850 buildings destroyed, c. 10,000 made homeless; the fire started during a violent storm.*
- *1906 – San Francisco earthquake and fire.* [192]

- *1906 – Dundee Fire of 1906, Scotland, began at a whiskey warehouse with alcohol explosions spreading flames, several blocks burned.*

The End of an Era - Good Bye to the Fire Horses

The "ad" below was placed in the New York Times with the following, "Once more, the picturesque is to yield to the utilitarian. That thrilling sight – three plunging horses drawing engine or hook and ladder – one of the few thrilling sights to be seen in our prosaic streets, is soon to become a thing of the past. Within the next five or six years, there will not be a fire horse in Greater New York. The gasoline motor will do the work of these old favorites."– New York Times, February 19, 1911

As much as there was resentment to the horses being brought into the firehouse, there was even more resentment to them being replaced by motorized vehicles. The firemen were fond of the horses and considered them part of the family. In Detroit, firefighters made fun of the chief's new vehicle and called it a "Hustle Buggy". Races were held between the horses and motorized vehicles. Sometimes the horses won but most times, the vehicles won. The argument to change was not only about the speed of the new vehicles but also about saving money. For instance, the Spokane, Washington Fire Department said the department's budget for maintenance would fall to $12,500 for the year compared to nearly $35,500 in 1911. It was the economy and efficiency that dictated the change. In Chicago it began in 1917 under the direction of John F. Cullerton, the fire department's business manager. Horses cost approximately $265.00 each and cost an additional $3,621.00 each on an average, per year to feed and care for. Motorized vehicles cost about $1,000.00 per vehicle per year to maintain. The savings in fire losses alone were estimated at about $1,000,000 annually. This was a direct result of the speed and efficiency in responding. Sometimes the vehicles broke down and mechanics were scarce in the beginning days of motorized transportation so some fire departments maintained a fleet of both motorized vehicles and horses for a while but eventually, all of the horses were retired. In Richmond, Indiana, when the first motorized fire truck was deployed in town in 1912, it crashed into the depot. It was then the horse-drawn fire wagons that first got to put out the blaze, beating the combustion engine vehicle. Nevertheless, motorized technology improved and horses were soon phased out.

Published in the The New York Times, Sunday, February 19, 1911. [157]

Last Runs - A Sad Farewell

FIRE DEPARTMENT OF NEW YORK

On December 20, 1922, at 10:15 am George W. Murray drove Balgriffen, Danny Beg, and Penrose on the final call for the last-horse-drawn engine in FDNY history. On the ash pan behind, Captain Leon Howard was keeping his hand on the whistle rope so that it screamed one long blast; Engineer Tom McEwen pushed coal into the firebox with both feet and one hand - he used his other hand to hold on tight. The muster ceremony ended as wreaths were placed on each horse and the press photos were taken. Then the 5 last fire horses of the FDNY were swapped for a new motorized engine and hose wagon. The old horse-drawn equipment would be sent to a small town or village and the horses were retired to a farm in upstate New York. (cited from: http://hatchingcatnyc.com/2015/01/24/last-horse-driven-engine-of-new-york-fire-department/)

Fire horses leave the quarters of FDNY Engine 39 and Ladder 16 on East 67th Street for the last time in 1911. Their replacement: the first gasoline-powered pumper, seen in the background. [158]

George W. Murray drives Balgriffen, Danny Beg, and Penrose on the final call for the last-horse-drawn engine in FDNY history. [159]

SAN FRANCISCO FIRE DEPARTMENT

The following article is from the July 11, 1912, San Francisco Chronicle.

Five panting foam-flecked horses, champions of their kind, drew up at the hydrant at Eleventh Avenue and Lake Street yesterday afternoon, losers in a race for existence. Two blocks away, a great red throbbing machine, a motor-driven fire engine, was churning away — an unsightly engine of modern development — a victor in that uneven race. It was a finish of a race between a modern motor-driven piece of fire apparatus and the horse-drawn apparatus of a day that has passed. The handicap of time was too great for the noble animals that for years have drawn heavy engines and carts loaded with hose to fires by day and by night.

"There will never be another piece of horse-drawn apparatus purchased for San Francisco," H.U. Brandenstein, president of the Board of Fire Commissioners, declared at the close of the race.

That was the verdict. When he made the remark the big glossy fire horses, nostrils distended as they breathed heavily from their exertion, stared wild-eyed at the great red machine a short distance away. They had raced madly behind that red car, but they couldn't overtake it. They plunged ahead with all their strength, but the red motor drew away from them and discharged its load of hose and men, and, with power of its gasoline driven pumps, was throwing water high in the air before the horses reached the hydrant with the heavy apparatus behind them.

A San Francisco Fire Department boiler rig and team in action. The horse teams were incredibly well trained and disciplined. Each fireman was assigned one horse to care for and the bonds between them were deep. Martin Murry Dunn was known throughout the Bay Area for breeding fine fire horses. [160]

It took the motor-driven combination fire engine and hose wagon just 2 minutes and 20 seconds to make the run from engine house No. 26, Second avenue and Clement street, to a hydrant at Thirteenth avenue and Lake street. It took the horse-drawn engine 3minutes and 55 seconds to cover the same distance. San Francisco replaced its last horse drawn steam engine in 1922. (cited from: https://www.sfchronicle.com/oursf/article/Our-SF-Fire-horses-doomed-after-losing-6601116.php)

SAN FRANCISO FIRE DEPARTMENT

On July 11, 1912, a contest between the horses and the new motorized trucks was held in front of San Francisco Fire Department Chief Thomas Murphy, the Fire Commissioners, the Fire Committee of the Board of Supervisors, and a large public crowd.

The best horse drawn engine in SFFD would race the new Nott Motor Engine to show which was the quickest and most effective. The contest started at 2nd Avenue & Clement Street, the home of 26 Engine. At the sound of a gong the horses bolted into their collars and ran out the door, dragging the smoking steamer. The Nott Motor Engine driver cranked the motor and quickly followed. The goal for the Nott Engine was to take the hydrant at 13th and Lake Streets. 2 minutes and 20 seconds later, the team had water flowing out the nozzle with a total elapsed time of 3 minutes and 40 seconds.

The steamer horses and team pulled up to the assigned hydrant at 11th and Lake Streets in 3 minutes and 55 seconds, and had water flowing in 5 minutes and 6 seconds. The results were painfully obvious - the days of the horses was over, and none were purchased following this event for fire department use. The first motor driven San Francisco Fire Department apparatus was installed in Chemical Company No. 3 on Bush Street in 1912. (cited from: https://www.marinfirehistory.org/the-transition-to-motorized-apparatus.html)

Displacing horse drawn for motor driven apparatus in the Quarters of Engine Company 21, Sept. 19, 1915. The presence of this firehouse in the late 1800s and early 1900s also marked the transition from horse-drawn carriages to fire engine machines—or as some would say, from "analog to digital". The huge earthquake and subsequent fire of 1906 marked a time when the majority of San Francisco firehouses were still using horse-drawn carriages to get to the scene of a fire. Firehouse No. 21 spent the majority of that time valiantly fighting fires in Hayes Valley for a whopping 54 hours. We found an old log at the library describing Firehouse No. 21's experiences that day: "The reports written just after the 1906 fire are fearsome tales. Captain H. Boden wrote that because the alarm and telephone systems which were not in order after the earthquake, they proceeded eastward "where we observed a column of smoke". They fought fire after fire, mostly in the Hayes Valley, trying again and again to obtain water. They finally returned to their station at 11:30am on April 20th, "having been on duty for fifty four hours". Besides Captain Boden, James Feeny, M. J. O'Connor, P.J. Meehan, W. Leonhardt, E. Long, T. Meacham, D. O'Connell and Charles Tyson fought these fires. [163]

PORTLAND FIRE DEPARTMENT

On May 13, 1929 - Portland Evening News Newspaper published the article, *Children Weep as Fire Horses Leave Engine 3 Station.*

Subtitle: Dan and Pete, beloved by Brackett street residents, retired to farm after six years of service; old Engine 4 is successor.

"Dan and Pete, coal black steeds that have for the past six years responded to fire alarms with the hose wagon at Engine three, Brackett Street, are the last of Portland's fire horses to be relegated to the ancient and honorable list with the coming of the motor pumper being transferred from Engine 4 on Tuesday.

Portland Engine 4, 1913. [161]

Farewells have all been said to the big black horses by more that a score of youngsters in the vicinity and tears were falling fast from the eyes of the kiddies in the neighborhood, at the loss of their friends.

Each night at nine o'clock it has been the habit of at least 20-juveniles to gather at the fire station at 8:59 to wait for the nine o'clock blows and see Dan and Pete run to the harness, set for a response to duty. After they are backed into the stable, the kids go to the stable door and fight for a place to watch the big boys make ready for the beds of straw, good-nights are shouted and the horses, seeming to know, nearly always respond with a whinnie.

The attraction of the animals for the children has never failed during the last six years. Their driver, Matthew J. Cady, tells of the fact that in one family there has never been a night in the season in which one or more of the same family has not been present at the goodnight period.

The children are not the only ones who are shedding tears for the loss of their equine friends, the eye of the Driver are dim, as he tells of the many unusual good points in the pair and the eyes of the listeners, who well know the love of man for beast are always somewhat showery. That the useful and intelligent animals will have a good home in their old age is a surety, as a well known gentleman, who is famous for his love for all animals, is said to be making negotiations for the ownership of not only Dan and Pete, the coal blacks of Engine Three's house, but also for Bill and Joe, the beautiful white pair, which were formerly stationed at Engine and Ladder Six at 292 Park Avenue."

CHICAGO FIRE DEPARTMENT

On February 6th, 1923 in Chicago, fire alarm box 846 at State and Chicago Avenue was pulled at 12:40 p.m. With the horses scrubbed and groomed, the old steamer rolled out of the swinging doors at Fire Engine 11 for the last time. Buck, Beauty, Dan and Teddy galloped out of the fire station at 10 E. Hubbard St. with their coach and the fire fighters riding on the engine. They were led by their Dalmatian escort to a false alarm. It was their last response. The alarm was pulled at a box at Chicago Avenue and State Street as part of a planned event to mark the retirement of the horse drawn engines and firefighting equipment in the City of Chicago. It was the first department in the United States with more than 500,000 residences to serve, to become completely motorized.

One of the city's last horse-drawn fire trucks on an alarm call, 1920, Chicago. [162]

While they were gone the new motor apparatus was backed into place, and the motorization of the Chicago Fire Department was an accomplished fact. The drivers took a cheer from the crowd on the return to the firehouse. Not everyone supported this change. One of the drivers, William Moir from Engine Company 105 wept as his horses were retired from service in 1922. "I never abused you, but I made you get over the ground," he told them as they were led away. "I feel like I've lost my best friends." Moir was twice decorated for saving lives in the line of duty. He joined the department because of his love of horses. He announced that he would quit the day his two "black beauties" were sent out to the pasture. But on that historic day in February in 1923, Chicago's Mayor Bill Thompson joined other dignitaries, the Chicago Fire Department's band, Fire Chiefs, firemen and their families, as well as thousands of spectators to watch the horses respond to their last fire bell. Buck, Beauty, Dan and Teddy answered their false alarm as if it were the real thing. They never returned to the station. (cited from: http://www.publicsafety.net/dalmatian.htm)

- 1907 – Hakodate, Hokkaido, Japan, a fire that broke out in the evening of August 25 burned for six hours, destroying an estimated 60–70% of the city, leaving 60,000+ homeless and causing at least 8,000,000 yen in property damage, including many of the city's historical buildings destroyed.
- 1908 – First Great Chelsea Fire on April 12. Nearly half the city of Chelsea, Massachusetts, was destroyed.
- 1909 – Phoenix, British Columbia destroyed by fire, then rebuilt.
- 1911 – Oscoda/AuSable, Michigan
- 1911 – Great Fire of 1911 in Bangor, Maine, destroyed hundreds of buildings.
- 1911 – Great Porcupine Fire in Porcupine, Ontario. Destroyed up to 494,000 acres of forest.
- 1912 – Houston, Texas, 56 city blocks; Houston's largest fire
- 1912 – Maryland Agricultural College, now the University of Maryland.
- 1914 – Great Salem Fire of 1914, Massachusetts. [193]

- 1916 – Bergen, Norway. About 300 buildings razed.
- 1916 – Matheson Fire, Matheson, Ontario. Destroyed approximately 490,000 acres of land.

DETROIT FIRE DEPARTMENT

The Detroit Fire Department acquired the first motorized fire engine in the world, a Packard. The last run of the Detroit Fire Horses took place down Woodward Avenue on August 3, 1922. More than 50,000 people gathered to witness the historic last run or Peter, Jim, Tom, Babe and Rusty, the horses of Engine 37's steamer and hose wagons.

Detroit Fire Horses ready for last run. [164]

They dashed down Woodward on a symbolic final emergency as a false alarm sounded at the National Bank Building. Nostalgic spectators lined Woodward from Grand Circus Park to Cadillac Square, cheering while the fire department's

Peter, Jim, Tom, Babe and Rusty, the horses of Engine 37's steamer and hose wagons dash down Woodward on a symbolic final emergency. [165]

band played Auld Lang Syne. According to The Detroit News, many in the crowd cried as the horses passed. The decision to replace the horses with mechanical vehicles met with a fury of objections by firefighters and Detroiters. It was argued that the horses were much more reliable. The motorized vehicles were hard starting and broke down too frequently. The firemen joked about the mechanical vehicles, nicknaming one the "Hustle Buggy." The debate over their beloved horses' replacement continued for several years. By 1908 there was no putting off the future. That year, the department unveiled its "Flying Squadron," a roomy Packard filled with fire extinguishers, axes, and a dozen firemen. It was "the fastest piece of human machinery in Detroit," an observer marveled, a "throbbing, clanging devil wagon" that hit speeds exceeding 40 mph while responding to alarms. Fourteen years after the purchase of the first Flying Squadron, the last 5 hooved firefighters retired to an "Equine Elysium" in Rouge Park. (cited from: http://www.dfdlegacy.com/detroit-fire-department-history-last-running-of-the-fire-horses/)

- *1916 – Paris, Texas Fire of 1916. Largest of 3 historical fires that destroyed most of the central business district and a large residential section.*
- *1917 – The Halifax Explosion, the largest man-made explosion before the atomic bomb, sparked fires throughout Halifax, Nova Scotia.*
- *1917 – Great Atlanta fire of 1917, during which over 300 acres (1.2 km2, 73 blocks) were destroyed.*
- *1917 – Great Thessaloniki Fire of 1917, Thessaloniki, Greece. About 9,500 buildings were destroyed.*
- *1917 – In Gyöngyös, Hungary, a fire destroyed a number of buildings, leaving around 8,000 people homeless.*
- *1920 – The Burning of Cork, Ireland, a fire set on December 11 by the British Auxiliaries in revenge after an ambush by the IRA destroyed much of the old city centre of Cork.*
- *1921 – Tulsa Race Riot resulted in the destruction of 35 city blocks and 1,256 residences by arson.*
- *1922 - The Fire of Manisa, Turkey*
- *1922 – The Great Fire of Smyrna, Izmir, Turkey*
- *1922 – Most of downtown Astoria, Oregon burns*
- *1922 – The Great Fire of 1922 in the Timiskaming District, Ontario, Canada, killed 43 people and burnt down 18 townships.*
- *1923 – 1923 Tokyo fire following the Great Kantō earthquake razed half the city with over 100,000 deaths.*
- *1923 – 1923 Berkeley Fire, California, destroyed at least 640 structures.*
- *1925 – 1925 Decatur St. Fire, Atlanta, Georgia, left 6 firefighters dead, 8 others seriously injured.*
- *1928 – Great Fall River fire of 1928, Massachusetts*

Firemen still tell stories of when fire horses "saved the day". Fire horses are remembered in toys and artwork and in everyone's hearts.

Cast-iron horse-drawn Steam Engine and Ladder Truck from the Gloria Austin Collection. Cast-iron toys, such as these horse-drawn Fire Apparatus dating from around 1900, reflect many commonplace but often forgotten aspects of everyday life. Hubley, Kentontoys, and Kingsbury Toys represented cast-iron toy manufacturers between the years of 1870s and 1960. Subjects include the circus, horse-drawn vehicles, public transportation, mail delivery, home equipment, recreation, construction equipment, the farm, fire fighting, and police vehicles. Cast-iron toys are essentially American. Small foundries and factories were mass-producing them towards the close of the 19th century. These toys were sold in novelty stores, department stores, or mail order catalogs. One can follow along with shifts in technology by recognizing the changes in the different models of Sears toys. During the first half of the 20th century, tractors almost completely displaced the horse on American farms—and on the toy counter. Toy motor trucks replaced horse-drawn vehicles. The toy manufacturers were alert to new models and designs of vehicle and appliance manufacturers. [168]

Horse drawn fire wagon and the new-fangled variety in one shot. The horses look less than impressed. Harold Stanfield photo, MCHS. [167]

There is nothing to it anymore. When they took the horses away, the pep and fun went out of the department. It was the sorriest day in our history." quoted one Baltimore fireman who quit the day the horses left the station.

Conclusion

As Loula Long Combs wrote in her book, My Revelation,

I wish I had the great gift of a painter of word pictures that I might be able to give you a faint idea of the most thrilling of all horse-drawn vehicles, the fire engine. It thrilled the very young as well as the very old. In the language of today, you who have never seen a horse-drawn fire engine, 'aint seen nuthin' (cited from: https://archive.org/stream/myrevelation027243mbp/myrevelation027243mbp_djvu.txt)

(above: 1911 Color postcard depicting a fire truck drawn by three horses, with ten firemen aboard. Printed on verso: The Detroit Fire Department is considered one of the best equipped in the country, and their promptness in responding to alarms is remarkable. The magnitude of the department is scarcely realized by the majority of the people. It requires the services of 630 men to handle the 32 engines, 13 trucks, 3 hose companies, 340 horses, 1 water tower and 2 fire boats.)

Firemen on Horse-Drawn Fire Truck, "On the Way to a Fire", Chicago, USA, Postcard, circa 1890 Front/Back. [170]

It's difficult to overestimate the degree to which the American economy and broader society revolved around horses. As one historian has commented, "every family in the United States in 1870 was directly or indirectly dependent on the horse." In rural areas, farmers prospered in no small measure by growing hay to feed the nation's 8.6 million horses, or one horse for every five people - and each horse ate a lot more than a person! In urban areas, the reliance was even more striking. This dependence hit home in the fall of 1872, when a serious strain of horse flu spread throughout the northeast U.S. and for some weeks horses could not be used. City life ground to a halt as streetcars stopped running, urban goods stopped moving, and construction sites stopped operating. Consumers suddenly confronted shortages when buying groceries. Perhaps even more disturbing for some, saloons ran out of beer. There was nothing like the horses' illness to demonstrate that such a large part of the American economy and its jobs revolved around horses. But beyond rural areas and big American cities, inventors were forging a new world, one which did not rely on horsepower. (cited from: https://blogs.microsoft.com/today-in-tech/day-horse-lost-job/)

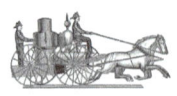

Sources

Books and periodicals

Ditzel, Paul C. (1976). Fire Engines Firefighters: The Men, Equipment, and Machines, from Colonial Days to the Present. New York, New York. Rutledge Books.

Levin, Jonathon V. (2017) Where Have All the Horse Gone? Jefferson, North Carolina. McFarland & Company, Inc.

Our Dumb Animals, Volume 50, No. 1, June 1917

Rhodes, J. A. (2006) The Fire Service History, Traditions and Beyond. Booklocker.com, Inc.

Smith, Dennis (1978) Dennis Smith's History of Firefighting in America. The Dial Press, New York

Hensler, Bruce (2011) Crucible of Fire. Potomac Books, Dulles, Virginia

Internet Sources

http://4.17.232.139/page.asp?mode=print&show=section&id=2819
http://americanhistory.si.edu/blog/hoof-fire-horse-number-12
http://antiqueshoppefl.com/articles/april06/fire%20fighters.htm
http://atomicstables.blogspot.com/2013/02/fire-department-harness-part-3-harness.html
http://atthefair.homestead.com/pkeatt/Halesfirefighter.html
http://blog.nyhistory.org/what-the-business-requires-images/
http://dagblog.com/reader-blogs/firefighting-and-capitalism-marcus-licinius-crassus-obion-county-tennessee-7092
http://emuseum.history.org/view/objects/asitem/2632/0?showSite=mobile
http://firehistory.weebly.com/a-history-of-horses-in-the-fire-service.html
http://guardiansofthecity.org/sffd/firehorses/chapter1.html
http://guardiansofthecity.org/sffd/fires/great_fires/1906/april_18_1906.html
http://hatchingcatnyc.com/2015/01/24/last-horse-driven-engine-of-new-york-fire-department/
http://hatchingcatnyc.com/2015/06/10/1912-victor-the-new-york-fire-horse-that-finally-lost-it-on-varick-street/
http://knowledgenuts.com/2014/05/02/when-firefighters-were-actually-violent-gang-members/
http://lishfd.org/History/firefighting_in_colonial_america.htm
http://northeastnews.net/pages/35332/
http://www.americanheritage.com/content/how-steam-blew-rowdies-out-fire-departments
http://www.ancientpages.com/2016/02/16/ancient-inventions-firefighting-vehicles/
http://www.craftcompany.com/firefighter.html
http://www.dfdlegacy.com/detroit-fire-department-history-last-running-of-the-fire-horses/
http://www.dps.state.ia.us/fm/inspection/history/History_of_Fire_and_Fire_Codes.pdf
http://www.equitrekking.com/articles/entry/famous_horses_in_history_-_the_fire_horse/
http://www.erinahose.com/history.htm
http://www.eyewitnesstohistory.com/rome.htm

http://www.firegold.com/2waterTower.html
http://www.firehorses.info/firehorsearticles.html
http://www.firemuseumcanada.com/the-addition-of-steam/
http://www.foresightguide.com/50CE-a-steam-engine-in-ancient-rome/
http://www.haverhillfirefightingmuseum.org/history-of-firefighting.php
http://www.kellscraft.com/GreatFireOfBoston/GreatFireofBostonCh02.html
http://www.lafire.com/archive/RulesRegulations/1901rules/index_rr1901.html
http://www.lafire.com/stations/fire_stations.htm
http://www.lastresortfd.org/SFD_History.htm
http://www.mi-harness.net/publct/tpr/firehorse.html
http://www.publicsafety.net/dalmatian.htm
http://www.toptenz.net/top-10-most-famous-fires-in-history.php
http://www.windsorfire.com/windsors-early-hose-wagons/
http://www.yorkblog.com/yorkspast/2015/12/29/exploits-mack/
http://yngfire.com/index.php?topic=2444.0
https://3milliondogs.com/dogbook/how-dalmatians-became-the-firehouse-mascot/
https://archive.org/stream/myrevelation027243mbp/myrevelation027243mbp_djvu.txt
https://blogs.microsoft.com/today-in-tech/day-horse-lost-job/
https://books.google.com/books?id=FJ-KmnMevWcC&pg=RA3-PA109&lpg=RA3-PA109&dq=detroit+fire+department+horse+bureau+allen+armstrong&source=bl&ots=9UERuGUrpD&sig=jjKkZZi4jG4-22DJofJw-sQpxiIg&hl=en&sa=X&ved=0ahUKEwiXoMLL8Y_aAhVP4mMKHYBoBQwQ6AEIQTAI#v=onepage&q=detroit%20fire%20department%20horse%20bureau%20allen%20armstrong&f=false
https://books.google.com/books?id=TCIDAAAAMBAJ&pg=PA617&lpg=PA617&dq=1871+-george+Hale+swinging+harness&source=bl&ots=UZjNcEeWtk&sig=UHjXITrRczcynU6J-J35gW-Z0EFs&hl=en&sa=X&ved=0ahUKEwiiuPCUiabaAhXKrlQKHWCvDjQQ6AEIMjAB#v=onepage&q=1871%20george%20Hale%20swinging%20harness&f=false
https://books.google.com/books?id=VKzhAAAAMAAJ&pg=PA155&lpg=PA155&dq=detroit+fire+department+horse+bureau+allen+armstrong&source=bl&ots=lGiaUSkVJ5&sig=WeTYxPRQSDimU78OZsd-QUarXBgg&hl=en&sa=X&ved=0ahUKEwiXoMLL8Y_aAhVP4mMKHYBoBQwQ6AEIPDAG#v=onepage&q&f=false
https://bostonfirehistory.org/fires/great-boston-fire-of-1872/
https://en.wikipedia.org/wiki/Great_Chicago_Fire
https://en.wikisource.org/wiki/Popular_Science_Monthly/Volume_47/September_1895/The_Development_of_American_Industries_Since_Columbus:_Fire_Fighting_II
https://forums.firehouse.com/forum/firefighting/firefighters-forum/63905-firefighting-history-timeline-1608-1909-input-wanted
https://legeros.com/history/horses/various.shtml

https://nypost.com/2007/11/16/the-great-fire-of-1835-3/
https://priceonomics.com/the-rise-and-fall-of-the-firemans-pole/
https://rear-view-mirror.com/2013/07/18/the-great-fire-of-rome-on-this-day-in-history/
https://www.americanheritage.com/content/tools
https://www.boston.com/news/history/2017/11/09/when-an-1872-fire-ravaged-downtown-boston
https://www.cincyfiremuseum.org/explore-the-museum/history/
https://www.doubledtrailers.com/13-fascinating-facts-about-horse-trailer-history/
https://www.firedex.com/blog/2011/10/21/early-fire-apparatus-the-horse-drawn-era/
https://www.firedex.com/blog/2014/02/19/george-washingtons-impact-fire-fighting/
https://www.firemarkcircle.org/documents/goodstory.htm
https://www.forbes.com/sites/drsarahbond/2017/07/18/july-18-64-the-great-fire-of-nero-and-the-ancient-history-of-firefighting/#28ea02aa9544
https://www.history.com/this-day-in-history/fire-rips-through-boston
https://www.history.com/this-day-in-history/great-fire-of-london-begins
https://www.history.com/topics/great-chicago-fire
https://www.lafra.org/lafd-history-hayes-aerial-ladder-truck/
https://www.marinfirehistory.org/the-transition-to-motorized-apparatus.html
https://www.massmoments.org/moment-details/boston-burns/submoment/boston-resolves-to-pay-firefighters.html
https://www.merrimacknh.gov/about-fire-rescue/pages/horses-in-fire-service
https://www.nps.gov/prsf/learn/historyculture/1906-earthquake-fire-fighting.htm
https://www.ourstate.com/new-bern-firemens-museum/
https://www.pal-item.com/story/news/local/2017/06/18/out-our-past-fire-department-used-rely-4-legged-heroes/405104001/
https://www.pal-item.com/story/news/local/2017/06/18/out-our-past-fire-department-used-rely-4-legged-heroes/405104001/
https://www.patersonfirehistory.com/horse-drawn-apparatus.html
https://www.portlandoregon.gov/fire/article/384861
https://www.revolvy.com/main/index.php?s=Great%20Boston%20Fire%20of%201760
https://www.sfchronicle.com/oursf/article/Our-SF-Fire-horses-doomed-after-losing-6601116.php
https://www.smithsonianmag.com/smithsonian-institution/early-19-century-firefighters-fought-fires-each-other-180960391/
https://www.thoughtco.com/new-yorks-great-fire-of-1835-
http://www.spokesman.com/stories/2017/apr/13/100-years-ago-in-spokane-fire-department-about-to-/#/0
https://en.wikipedia.org/wiki/List_of_town_and_city_fires

Image Sources

1 Fire insurance https://www.loc.gov/resource/pga.13893/ Print shows fire fighters manning firehoses and pump wagons at a fire in a commercial building or warehouse, as other men attempt to salvage property from the burning building. At right center is a statue of a female figure standing on a pedestal emblazoned with a shield showing symbols of commerce, she is holding a pike on which is a banner that states "Indemnity"; at her feet is a large eagle. Kneass, William, 1780-1840, engraver

1a Rome fire, Robert, Hubert - Incendie à Rome - By Hubert Robert - http://www.kunst-fuer-alle.de/index.php?mid=77&lid=1&blink=76&stext=caesar&cmstitle=Bilder,-Kunstdrucke,-Poster:-Caesar&start=80, Public Domain, https://commons.wikimedia.org/w/index.php?curid=6606073

1b The Great Fire of London, depicted by an unknown painter, 1675. "This painting shows the great fire of London as seen from a boat in vicinity of Tower Wharf. The painting depicts Old London Bridge, various houses, a drawbridge and wooden parapet, the churches of St Dunstan-in-the-West and St Bride's, All Hallow's the Great, Old St Paul's, St Magnus the Martyr, St Lawrence Pountney, St Mary-le-Bow, St Dunstan-in-the East and Tower of London. The painting is in the [style] of the Dutch School and is not dated or signed." By Josepha Jane Battlehooke - museumoflondonprints.com, Public Domain, https://commons.wikimedia.org/w/index.php?curid=1303944

Additions Sources for London fire:
- Political climate during the London Fire (1666) of History of England from the Accession of James II, Vol I by Thomas Babington Macaulay, Hannah Trevelyan (1850) London: Longman, Brown, Green, Longmans, and Roberts.pg 192
- Papist blamed for fire in London, 1693 of History of England from the Accession of James II, Vol IV by Thomas Babington Macaulay (1856), Philadelphia: Published by E. H. Butler & Co. pg 353
- Samuel Pepys diary entry on London fire Sunday, Sept 2, 1666. https://www.pepysdiary.com/diary/1666/09/02/
- Robert Hubert - frenchman said to start fire, plus other thoeories https://www.pepysdiary.com/encyclopedia/10872/
- Samuel Pepys entry on London fire Sunday, Feb 24, 1667. - https://www.pepysdiary.com/diary/1667/02/24/
- In 1986, London's bakers finally apologized to the lord mayor for setting fire to the city. Members of the Worshipful Company of Bakers gathered on Pudding Lane and unveiled a plaque acknowledging that one of their own, Thomas Farrinor, was guilty of causing the Great Fire of 1666. https://www.history.com/this-day-in-history/great-fire-of-london-begins
- Cestui Que Vie Act 1666 https://www.legislation.gov.uk/aep/Cha2/18-19/11

An Act for Redresse of Inconveniencies by want of Proofe of the Deceases of Persons beyond the Seas or absenting themselves, upon whose Lives Estates doe depend. X1Recital that Cestui que vies have gone beyond Sea, and that Reversioners cannot find out whether they are alive or dead. [I.]Cestui que vie remaining beyond Sea for Seven Years together and no Proof of their Lives, Judge in Action to direct a Verdict as though Cestui que vie were dead. IVIf the supposed dead Man prove to be alive, then the Title is revested. Action for mean Profits with Interest.

- When London burned, the subrogation of men's and women's rights occurred. The responsible act passed... CQV act 1666 meant all men and women of UK were declared dead and lost beyond the seas. The state took everybody and everybody's property into trust. The state takes control until a living man or woman comes back and claims their titles by proving they are alive and claims for damages can be made. This is why you always need representation when involved in legal matters, because you're dead. https://areweallreallyeducated.com/the-cestui-que-vie-act-of-1666/

1c The Angel of Death Flying Over the Great Boston Fire. Woodcut by Zechariah Fowle and Samuel Draper, 1760. https://guides.bpl.org/bostonfires

1d View of the Great Fire in New York, December 16th – 17th, 1835 by Nicolino Calyo. https://www.schwarzgallery.com/artist/nicolino-calyo/

1e The Chicago Fire, 1871. By Miscellaneous Items in High Demand, PPOC, Library of Congress
- Library of CongressCatalog: https://lccn.loc.gov/2016647669Image download: https://cdn.loc.gov/service/pnp/cph/3a40000/3a40000/3a40600/3a40633r.jpgOriginal url: https://www.loc.gov/pictures/

item/2016647669/, Public Domain, https://commons.wikimedia.org/w/index.php?curid=68047077

1f Federal Street Post Office in the wake of the Great Boston Fire of 1872. One of the Bictorian fire pumpers, like the Kearsarge of Portsmouth, employed at the Great Fire of Boston on Nov. 9-10. The blaze destroyed 776 buildings on 65 acres over 12 hours. (Boston Public Library)

1g Fire in San Francisco following the great earthquake of 1906. View if from Gold Gate Park, Marin County, California. (USGS) By George R. Lawrence - USGS via The Atlantic https://www.theatlantic.com/photo/2016/04/photos-of-the-1906-san-francisco-earthquake/477750/, Public Domain, https://commons.wikimedia.org/w/index.php?curid=74032311

1h Lloyd's subscription room: This engraving was published as Plate 49 of Microcosm of London (1809) By Thomas Rowlandson (1756–1827) and Augustus Charles Pugin (1762–1832) (after) John Bluck (fl. 1791–1819), Joseph Constantine Stadler (fl. 1780–1812), Thomas Sutherland (1785–1838), J. Hill, and Harraden (aquatint engravers) - see above, Public Domain, https://commons.wikimedia.org/w/index.php?curid=594862

2 This graphic depicts a young George Washington pulling a wooden fire pumper. Later, as President, Washington often took the time to visit local fire companies; inquiring about developments in apparatus and talking with the firemen. http://educationaltour.fasnyfiremuseum.com/1700-george-washington.html

3 Portrait of Alexander Hamilton (1757-1804) by John Trumbull

4 John Hancock, Painting by John Singleton Copley

5 Portrait drawing of Massachusetts patriot Samuel Adams.by Jacques Reich (based on an earlier work by J. S. Copley) By Jacques Reich (based on an earlier work by J. S. Copley) - Appletons' Cyclopædia of American Biography, v. 1, 1900, p. 29, Public Domain, https://commons.wikimedia.org/w/index.php?curid=14993677

6 Paul Revere Portrait - John Singleton Copley 1768

7 A political cartoon depicting the Plug Uglies of Baltimore, MD, originally the Mount Vernon Hook and Ladder Volunteer Fire Company during the 1856 riots. https://www.coffeeordie.com/baltimore-fire-department-gangs or By Cartoon of Mobtown, Collection of the Maryland Historical Society; Maryland State Archives, Public Domain, https://commons.wikimedia.org/w/index.php?curid=94900061

8 Cincinnati's first steam-powered fire engine was named the "Uncle Joe Ross" after the city councilman who introduced legislation to buy the pumper for the city. From history of the Cincinnati Fire Department, 1895 digitized by public library of Cincinnati & Hamilton County or https://www.cincinnatimagazine.com/article/the-curious-and-explosive-history-of-cincinnatis-first-steam-fire-engine/

9 Volunteer Fire Department, Pittsburgh, Oct 1907. Mercer Museum and Fontill Castle Collection, Doylestown, PA. https://www.mercermuseum.org/event/exhibit-to-save-our-fellow-citizens-volunteer-firefighting-1800-1875/ and http://www.firegold.com/firemenArtist.html

10 Ctesibio: Greek Inventor and Father of Pneumatics, Se considera padre de la neumática al genio de origen griego, Ctesibio (285 – 222 a.C.), gran inventor y matemático griego. Ctesibio's Pump - With one of his great inventions he has laid the foundations for our current work: Ctesibio's Pump. Also known as the Fire Extinguishing Pump and described both in Vitruvio's "De architectura" Book X and in the writings of Heron of Alexandria. Ctesibio's Pump, of which there is a fairly well-preserved unit in the National Archaeological Museum, consists of a pump equipped with 4 valves and two chambers or pistons that pump water at high pressure through an adjustable nozzle. It is easy to interpret that this operating scheme corresponds directly to the mechanism used in a modern double diaphragm pneumatic pump. Therefore, we can proudly point out that the pumping machines we use today were invented more than 2,000 years ago by the mind of a great inventor – Ctesibio! https://www.followthefluid.com/happy-international-inventors-day-from-samoa/?lang=en In the 2nd century BC Ctesibius's devised a force pump. - On each side was a piston raised by a rocking handle, which sucked water into a cylinder through a one-way valve. By pushing the piston down, the water was forced into the outlet pipe. The Romans adapted the device to drain bilges, extinguish fires and feed fountains. http://www.jesusneverexisted.com/lost-world2.html

11 How the pump invented by Ctesibius works (drawing by Tamás Lajtos) Ctesibius's other important idea was the piston-pump, which could be used for raising water. His invention also became widely used in practice; its description survives in the accounts of Vitruvius and Heron, hence the device is known

by posterity as the pump of Heron. Just how ingenious the invention was is shown by the fact that it was used not only in Antiquity and the Middle Ages; fire pumps until the 19th century operated based on the same principle. Furthermore, piston pumps and compressors are still in use today in several areas of industry. According to a 1615 book by Venetian architect Vincenzo Scamozzi, a pump of this kind was also used to bring water to the Buda Castle. http://www.aquincum.hu/en/blog/ktesibios/

12 Cohort VII Vigiles - Their structure and organization in some ways resembles the current organization of the fire brigade, which, however, in addition to the fires, should also have provided for the night police against arsonists, burglars, thieves and so on. Augustus, who had divided the city of Rome into fourteen regions, placed each of them under the control of seven cohortes, made up of about 1000 men each who stayed in barracks, called statio, and guard posts or detachments, known as excubitorium. The presence of barracks and guard posts, of men preeminently residing in the barracks and specifically assigned to the prevention and suppression of fires, together with the tasks of the city police, made this Militia a very advanced organization for the time. The vigiles had a paramilitary organization; they were framed in seven cohorts subdivided in turn into seven centuries each, each comprising a hundred men at the head of which was the centurion. Therefore each cohort had to ensure service in the territory of two regions and had a barracks (statio) in one of them and a detachment, a guardhouse (excubitorium) in the other. Each cohort was commanded by a tribunus, just as at the head of the centuries was a centurion, flanked by the non-commissioned officers adiutores centurionis. https://www.romanoimpero.com/2011/03/vigiles-romani.html

13 Roman Pump - CAUS, Solomon of (1576-1626). The reasons for the shifting forces with various machines both useful and pleasant. Paris: Hierosme Drouärt, 1624. https://www.christies.com/lot/lot-caus-salomon-de-1576-1626-les-raisons-des-6040792/

14 1793 Fire Bucket Leather - This leather fire bucket is purported to have once belonged to Henry Knox. The inventory of items that he shipped from Philadelphia to Thomaston does include fire buckets, and this may be one of those. Underneath the painted eagle is the year 1793. The painting is unsigned. Donated to Montpelier by an unknown source. Accession number: P-020 https://knoxmuseum.org/portfolio-posts/leather-fire-bucket-1793/

15 Richard Newsham's patented "4th size" hand pump fire engine. A coiled leather hose, a hard hose, miscellaneous fittings and 3 fire buckets (1960-236, 2 thru 1960-236, 8) remain with the fire engine since its period of use. https://emuseum.history.org/view/objects/asitem/items$0040:16279

16 Fire Extinguishher - https://sandiegohistory.org/journal/1989/april/eating/ Early fire extinguishers were primitive, ineffective, and sometimes dangerous.

17 Leather hose - Very Early LEATHER Fire Hose. In very Good Condition with nozzle and hydrant connectors. https://www.icollector.com/Very-Early-LEATHER-Fire-Hose_i10334585

18 Hose cart/hose cart race/hose cart - https://www.marinfirehistory.org/hose-cart-racing.html

19 The Larkspur VFD Team - https://www.marinfirehistory.org/hose-cart-racing.html

20 The Saugatuck Fire Department in Michigan, in a good photo showing both fire buckets and hose carts. Photo courtesy Saugatuck-Douglas Historical Society.

21 Log with plug - A wooden fire main with several fire plugs. The holes were cut into the logs to get water to fight the fire, and the plugs would later be installed to stop the leak. Eventually metal pipes and above ground hydrants would be developed. https://www.marinfirehistory.org/hose-cart-racing.html A piece of history was recently found under the streets of Portland. Pictured here is a section of a wooden water main, aka a hollowed out log. Firefighters would have to dig a hole to reach the pipe, then drill through the wooden pipe to intentionally create a leak. The hole would fill with water so the fire engines could pump it out. This brings an all new meaning to the term "Shoveling hydrants"! After the incident the firefighters would seal the hole with a wooden plug, hence the term "fire plug". Photo ctsy Portland Water Dist. https://m.facebook.com/local1476/photos/a-piece-of-history-was-recently-found-under-the-streets-of-portland-pictured-her/1760809557510017/

22 Wood planks - A wood-stave pipe. As early as the late 1800's they were building continuous wood-stave pipes in the 12 and 14 feet diameter size for literally miles of water transfers. Instead of all being the same length and built flush with each other, this construction method staggered the staves so that pipe building would just go on and on until you got to where you were going. https://nwksgmd4.blogspot.com/2012/09/remember-wooden-water-pipes.html

23 Elm water pipes - Elm water pipes being excavated in Gosport High Street in 1936; these were well

over 200 years old when dug up. http://www.gosportheritage.co.uk/11-bury-cross-waterworks/elm-water-pipes-being-excavated-in-gosport-high-street-in-1936-these-were-well-over-200-years-old-when-dug-up/

24 Napoleon House, New Orleans, Louisiana. Photo c. 1900 - 1906. View from across intersection of Chartres & St. Louis Streets. A horse-drawn ice wagon seen on Chartres Street. In front of the head of the horse, a wooden fire-plug (ancestor of the metal fire hydrant) is seen embedded in the sidewalk at the curb. Balcony of the old St. Louis Hotel seen at left of photo. By Unnamed photographer for Detroit Publishing Company - Detroit Publishing Company Photograph Collection via Library of Congress website [1]. Converted from TIFF to .jpg, border cropped, and slight contrast adjusted before uploading to Wikimedia Commons., Public Domain, https://commons.wikimedia.org/w/index.php?curid=9396005

25 Red fire alarm - By Ben Schumin - Own work, CC BY-SA 2.5, https://commons.wikimedia.org/w/index.php?curid=1035868

26 Wooden fire alarm - https://www.worthpoint.com/worthopedia/gamewell-antique-fire-alarm-visual-412799469

27 Fireboat Three Forty Three of Marine Company 1, FDNY's largest fireboat. By Peter Stehlik - PS-2507 - Own work, CC BY 3.0, https://commons.wikimedia.org/w/index.php?curid=20086193

28 March 1, 1890 - Scientific American, A weekly journal of practical information, art, science, mechanics, chemistry, and manufactures. Vol. LXII. Est. 1845. New York, NY. Download a copy at https://ia801506.us.archive.org/20/items/scientific-american-1890-03-01/scientific-american-v62-n09-1890-03-01.pdf

THE NEW BOSTON FIRE BOAT " ENGINE NO. 3!."

The city of Boston has recently built and put into service a fire boat, designed for use as a floating fire engine. As the vessel in question represents the most advanced type of fire boat, and in a number of points differs from any hitherto constructed, we illustrate it in this issue. The construction of boats of this kind has now been developed until they are no longer mere tug boats with special pumps. Everything in their design is intended to insure the production of a true floating fire engine, one that for days in succession, without a minute's intermission, can throw water upon burning buildings or shipping. Thus on the occasion of the burning of the great elevators of the New York Central Railroad in this city, in May, 1889, the New York Fire Department boat Havemeyer was kept at work for nineteen days and nights, her boiler being under forced draught for that period. This, of course, was a highly exceptional occurrence. There are but few structures in New York and its environs that would require such heroic treatment if burning. Yet it shows what a fire boat may be called on to perform.

The new Boston fire boat is named "Engine No. 31," and has no other title. The general dimensions are as follows : Length over all, 108 feet ; on water line, 97 feet ; beam, maximum, 24½ feet ; on water line, 23 feet : depth of hold, 8 feet 1 inch ; draught, 7 feet 4 inches. The hull is of wood, and is of extra strength to resist the exceptionally heavy strains to which the heavy machinery will subject it. The best quality of white oak is used for the principal members of the frame and for the plan king. Hackmatack and yellow pine are used for upper frames and other parts. Below the waterline the hull is sheathed with yellow metal.

The stem under the water curves upward very gradually from the keel, and from a point about two feet above the water line downward and aft for about twenty feet carries a yellow metal shoe, one-half inch thick. On the hurricane deck, or above the main deck house, is the pilot house and the officers' house and drying room. The cabins in the main deck house include officers' cabin and main cabin, galley, mess room, and general offices. Accommodations for a crew of fourteen wen and officers are provided in this house.

The steam is generated by Cowles' water tube boilers. There are two of these, each occupying an area of 11½ X 7⅓ feet, and in height rising 11½ feet. When filled with water and ready for use the two weigh 19 '74 tons. They have 3,200 square feet of heating surface, a little over 87 square feet of grate'surface, and are tested up to 300 pounds, giving a working allowance of 200 pounds. With natural draught they develop 400 horse power, which may, by steam jets in the chimney, be brought up to 900 horse power. This boiler is a sort of combination tube and shell boiler. The tube ends are expanded into place, so that no screw connections are exposed to the fire. The same type of boiler is used upon the New York fire boat Havemeyer.

The engine is two·cylinder compound, 18 and 34 inch cylinders, with 20 inch stroke. They are inverted, and are carried on six wrought iron columns. They have link gear, and in general are of the tug boat type. A Wheeler surface condenser of 1,000 square feet surface is employed to condense the exhaust steam. The shaft is of wrought iron and steel, and is 6¾" inches diameter at its smallest part. Steam reversing gear is used.

Two screws are used, embodying the Kunstadter steering gear arrangement. One works just aft of the stern

post and forward of the rudder, in the usual place. The other, termed the swiveling screw, is carried by a short shaft journaled in the rudder, and revolves about this as an axis, the rudder being cut away to allow it to rotate. This short shaft is connected to the main shaft by a universal joint directly in line with the rudder post, which is cut away to allow room for it to work in. As the rudder turns, it turns the axis of the after screw, so as to materially re-enforce the directive action of the rudder. The rudder is of cast steel. The front screw is of 6 ft. diameter and 9 ft. pitch; the after or swiveling screw is of the same diameter, but of 10 ft. pitch. Each has four cast steel blades. When the rudder is straight, the thrust of both screws comes upon the inboard thrust bearings; when the rudder is inclined, the oblique component of the thrust of the after screw is taken by the rudder frame.

A steam steering engine, double cylinder, 7 in. stroke, 5 in. diameter, is employed to turn the rudder and the swiveling screw. A small steering wheel in the pilot house is used for working it. Spare tackle is provided for steering by tiller when necessary.

The pumps were built by the Clapp & Jones Manufacturing Company, of Hudson, N.Y. They are of vertical, duplex, double-acting flywheel type. They are divided into two sets, comprising altogether 4 steam cylinders, 10 in. by 10 in., and 4 water cylinders of 10 in. stroke and 9 in. diameter. One set is placed on each side of the engine room. In the forward end of the deck house is a cast iron 12 inch header, into which the pumps force their discharge. It has four 3½ in. and four 2½ in. hose connections, with gates or valves. To these hose of any length may be connected, so that water can be delivered at high pressure, one or two thousand feet away. Upon the forward deck are also installed two Cowles swiveled nozzles carried by short stand pipes. Each of these delivers a four inch stream of water. They can swing through a complete circle, and can be elevated 60 degrees. A 9½ in. copper pipe is carried from the pumps below deck on the port side, to supply the header and stand pipes. The means for perfectly controlling these immense streams are well illustrated in the cut. The maximum working pressure is 225 lb. On the trials this pressure was not attained. The pumps could be driven up to 320 and 330 revolutions per minute. At 300 revolutions, with 50 to 60 lb. pressure, they worked well. A good working speed was found to be 210 revolutions and 140 lb. pressure. They threw a 4 in. stream from the Cowles nozzle about 400 ft. and four $2\frac{5}{8}$ streams 230 ft. through 100 ft. of 3¼ in. hose and hand pipes simultaneously.

On her trial trips the boat was found to be of good speed, developing a speed of 16 2-7 statute miles per hour. The swiveling screw on this speed test showed a slip of only 4'7 per cent, and the leading or stationary screw showed a negative slip, due undoubtedly to the boat drawing water after it. A considerable slip is not incompatible with efficiency, and the old view that the two could not coexist has been abandoned.

The fire pumps were found to be unexceptionable in their working. In the illustration a good idea is given of the service that such a boat can perform. In addition to the two four-inch streams thrown from her forward deck under perfect control, a number of lines of hose can be carried from the header, so as to deliver water to engines on shore. Thus the boat is not merely for the protection of the water front. Most useful service can be executed in a belt 2,000 feet wide around the shore line.

High speed is a valuable factor in boats of this character, as enabling the nearest point to a conflagration to be quickly reached. This is possessed by .. Engine 31." The Kunstadter screw steering attachment increases the maneuvering powers greatly. A positive and efficient steering can be obtained when the engines are reversed, so that the boat can be worked to a certain extent as a double ender. This quality of good steering when going backward might be of the utmost importance in critical positions.

29 For 40 years, "The New Yorker" stood guard over the New York Harbor. The battle-scarred veteran was the first fireboat to have a permanent shore station at Pier I, N.R. THE NEW YORKER was constructed by Julius Jonson, New York, from plans by Charles H. Haswell. With a pumping capacity of 13,000 gpm, she was for many years the most powerful of fireboats. She was the first New York fireboat with a shore station and its house at the Battery became a landmark as famous as the boat itself. When THE NEW YORKER was ready, Engine Co. 57 was organized and the boat placed in service on February 1, 1891. News articles of the day gave much space to descriptions of the boat and its architecturally distinctive station near Castle Garden. She had a steel hull and a profile which was changed some years later by the installation of a larger stack and the removal of some of the superstructure. She was a single screw vessel with a triple expansion engine. On January 24, 1892, the ZOPHAR MILLS collided with THE NEW YORKER, hitting her head-on near the water line on the port side during a heavy fog. The crew were able to keep her pumped out until she could be berthed at a shipyard. In those memorable winters of the 1890's, ice in the rivers around New York was a menace to the fireboats. On

February 13, 1899, the DAVID A. BOODY sank in the East River at the foot of Corlears Street, while returning from a fire. The Captain sent out a call for help and the crew strove desperately to pump her out, hut to avail. The same day, the VAN WYCK damaged her steering gear and was towed to her berth by THE NEW YORKER.http://marine1fdny.com/fireboat_history_new.php, https://www.digitalcommonwealth.org/search/commonwealth:05742d16b, Fire boats fighting five alarm Charlestown fire, 1930.

30 Pompier Ladder - French-made scaling ladders. The top of the ladder, with its iron catch, would be hooked over a window sill, and the firefighter would climb the narrow rungs to the window. He would stand on the sill and pull the ladder up and raise it to the next window and repeat the process. http://fire-men-book.blogspot.com/2013/04/old-school-rescue-history-lesson.html

31 Boston FF's demonstrating the use of pompier ladders in 1935. Although these ladders are rarely used today, all Boston FF's must be proficient in their use. It is one of the last evolutions BFD Recruits must complete to graduate. It is a BFD tradition & confidence builder. https://twitter.com/bostonfire/status/1006203395185807361

32 The Life of a Fireman - The Night Alarm Currier and Ives circa 1854, D'Amour Museum of Fine Arts - Team of firemen pulling wagon out of building and headed to right down street in image. Louis Maurer, American, 1832-1932 Throughout his prints of fire fighting, Louis Maurer emphasized accuracy. Here, a group of firemen from Excelsior Company No. 2, of 21 Henry Street, New York City, are shown pulling a pumper-wagon from the firehouse in response to a night alarm. The clock inside the firehouse reads 1:22. At the left, Nathaniel Currier, a volunteer fire fighter with the company, runs to join his colleagues, James Merritt Ives and George B. Ives. This print is one in a series of six that was produced to acknowledge the bravery of fire fighters. https://springfieldmuseums.org/collections/item/the-life-of-a-fireman-the-night-alarm-nathaniel-currier/

33 History of the Bellevue Fire Department https://fdbd.org/about-fdbd/history/history-of-the-bellevue-fire-department/

34 The first horse purchased for the department was "Old Kit" and soon after, two more horses were purchased. It has been said Old Kit could take a corner going 60 miles an hour. http://www.cityofgloversville.com/old-kit/

35 Union Engine No. 3 - York, Pa., fire department, 1910-1920 https://www.loc.gov/item/90710335/

36 Steam Engine Ad - Ahrens-Fox Fire Engine Co Cincinnati Ohio 1910-1977 http://cincinnatitriplesteam.org/ahrens-fox.htm

37 1894 Silsby Fourth Size Horse-Drawn Steam Pumper, https://www.car-revs-daily.com/2016/04/09/1894-silsby-horse-drawn-steam-fire-engine/

38 Fire Department. Newton, MA. Horse-drawn engine [ca. 1880–1995] https://www.digitalcommonwealth.org/search/commonwealth:2227mv52d

39 Horse-drawn two wheeled hose reel .Union Engine No. 3 - York, Pa., fire department, 1910-1920 https://www.loc.gov/item/90710335/

40 Horse-drawn four wheeled hose reel. 1900 at Station 7 - 15th Ave E & E Harrison St. Seattle, WA. http://www.lastresortfd.org/SFD_History.htm

41 Combination Hose and Chemical Wagon, #3 Battle Creek, Michigan.

42 Horse-drawn four wheeled hose wagon once in the Gloria Austin Collection.

43 Horse-Drawn Chemical Engine #1, 1889 Champion w/two 80-Gallon Soda-Acid Chemical Tanks (Served at Chemical 1, 3 and 33) Photo taken: 1900 at Station 1 - 7th Ave & Columbia St. http://www.lastresortfd.org/SFD_History.htm

43a Horse-Drawn Chemical Engine #2, 1890 Holloway w/two 50-Gallon Soda-Acid Chemical Tanks. Rebuilt in 1901 as Hose-Chemical Combination w/one 50-Gallon Soda-Acid Chemical Tank (Served at Chemical 2, Combination 2 & E-8's Hose Wagon) Shown here as Chemical 2, Photo taken: 1900 at Chemical Engine House #2 - Broadway & Terrace St., Sold after 1907 - current status unknown. http://www.lastresortfd.org/SFD_History.htm#____Chemical%20Engines

44 Chemical Truck #1 - Wash. - Wenatchee - Wenatchee Fire Dept, 1911; https://www.loc.gov/item/2007678209/

44a SFD Temporary Quarters of Chemical 1 (1889-1890), Western Ave (West St) & Spring St., Photo taken: 1890, Structure temporarily occupied 6 months after Great Seattle Fire of June 6, 1889. Occupied until July, 1890 when Chemical 1 moved into temporary Headquarters shown above. Torn down: Unknown. Current use of property: Commercial structure - Central Business District. http://www.lastresortfd.org/SFD_History.htm

45 Horse-drawn Chemical Unit Truck once in the Gloria Austin Collection.

46 Photograph shows a fire at the George J. Mueller Candy Co., 336 Pennsylvania Ave.,

NW, in Chinatown, Washington. (Source: Library staff and Arlington Fire Journal and Metro D.C. Fire History: http://arlingtonfirejournal.blogspot.com/2019/08/chinatown-1925.html) and https://www.loc.gov/resource/npcc.15344/

47 Remarkable fire at coal yard, South Boston, with water tower in action (115-F) 1911. https://www.digitalcommonwealth.org/search/commonwealth:0p0968280

48 Horse-Drawn Water Tower #1 - 1904 Champion 65' Water Tower with 1100 GPM Monitor at Station 10 - 3rd Ave S & S Main St. Seattle, WA. http://www.lastresortfd.org/SFD_History.htm

49 Horse-drawn ladder truck from a Seagrave factory photo. Close up of a curved hook and a flat hook on a ladder truck, 1890's. Master historian Matt Lee included this picture in his 1997 book "A Pictorial History of the Fire Engine – Volume I."[1] Horse-drawn ladder truck with "T. F. D." on the side. https://legeros.com/blog/hooks-and-ladders/

50 LAFD History – The Hayes Aerial Ladder Truck - The Hayes 65 foot Aerial Ladder Truck began service as a Volunteer Company in 1884 known as the Vigilance Hook & Ladder No. 1, located downtown at Aliso and Alameda. https://www.lafra.org/lafd-history-hayes-aerial-ladder-truck/

51 Horse-Drawn 1889 Preston 65' Aerial Ladder Truck #8. Aerial shortened to 55' in 1911. 1912 at Station 18 - Russell Ave NW & NW Market St. Seattle, WA. http://www.lastresortfd.org/SFD_History.htm#___Ladder%20Trucks

52 Horse-Drawn 1906 American LaFrance 85' Tillered Aerial Ladder Truck#2 Photo taken: 1907 at Station 10 - 3rd Ave S & S Main St. Seattle, WA. http://www.lastresortfd.org/SFD_History.htm#___Ladder%20Trucks

53 Ladder Truck at the George J. Mueller Candy Company in Chinatown, WA, 1925. https://www.loc.gov/resource/npcc.15344/

54 American LaFrance Hayes Aerial Ladder (1902) https://www.miniworlds.de/feuerwehr_usa_ny.html

55 Horse-Drawn Chief's Buggy - Between 1909 & 1913 at Station 4 - 4th Ave N & Thomas St. Seattle, WA. http://www.lastresortfd.org/SFD_History.htm#Chiefs%20Buggies

56 Horse-drawn Chief's Buggy once in the Gloria Austin Collection.

57 Horseshoeing equipment - 1916 at Station 25 - Harvard Ave & E Union St. Seattle, WA. http://www.lastresortfd.org/SFD_History.htm

58 Supply Wagon - 1900 at Station 2 - 3rd Ave & Pine St. Seattle, WA. http://www.lastresortfd.org/SFD_History.htm

59 Photograph shows the aftermath of the Great Fire of 1911 in Bangor, Maine which took place on April 30 and May 1, 1911. (Source: Flickr Commons project, 2015) https://www.loc.gov/resource/ggbain.09168/

60 A woman driving a wagon and horses in north London during the first world war. The picture was taken on 16 August 1916. https://www.theguardian.com/artanddesign/gallery/2013/sep/21/photography-first-world-war-women

61 Insurance Patrol - https://chicagofirepatrol.com/Chicago_Fire_Insurance_Patr.html

62 First horse ambulance invented in 1867 in NYC, Images from ASPCA website. https://amesburycarriagemuseum.org/news/2022/6/26/youth-amp-family-news-what-happened-when-there-were-too-many-horse-driven-carriages-in-cities

62a Besides transporting racehorses, many of the very first horse trailers were actually horse-drawn ambulances used by city fire departments. Horse injuries were common at city accidents and they needed a way to quickly transport wounded but savable horses back to the firehouse for veterinary care. https://www.doubledtrailers.com/13-fascinating-facts-about-horse-trailer-history/

63 Hose, wagon, and horses ready for call in 1910. (OKCFD) OKLAHOMA CITY (KOKH) — Did you know Oklahoma City Fire Department began as a small volunteer organization. https://okcfox.com/news/local/the-history-of-the-oklahoma-city-fire-department

64 Interior, apparatus floor, quick hitch system suspended from ceiling, New York Engine Co. 76, 1907. PR 63. https://www.nyhistory.org/blogs/what-the-business-requires-images

65 Hitching up the fire horses, Hook and Ladder Co. 25, 1906. PR 63. https://www.nyhistory.org/blogs/what-the-business-requires-images

66 Quick Hitch Collar once on display in the Gloria Austin Collection. https://www.equineheritageinstitute.com/

67 Ad fo the Hale Swinging Harness with Adjustable Collar and Hames https://www.digitalcommonwealth.org/search/commonwealth:j67318369

68 Ad for accessory to improve the operation of the Quick Hitch Harness. https://www.forestparkreview.com/2016/10/18/horse-harness-brings-back-memories-of-big-jim/

69 Various Horse Drawn Fire Apparatus once on display in the Gloria Austin Collection. https://www.

equineheritageinstitute.com/

70 Various Horse Drawn Fire Apparatus once on display in the Gloria Austin Collection. https://www.equineheritageinstitute.com/

71 The Rise and Fall of the Fireman's Pole, https://priceonomics.com/the-rise-and-fall-of-the-firemans-pole/ Interior view of (probably) fire station number 5 (Five) in Denver, Colorado; men by iron beds pull pants on over long underwear. Two men slide on poles into holes in the floor, 1905. https://cdm16079.contentdm.oclc.org/digital/collection/p15330coll22/id/66409

72-75 The present (1901) departments consists of one hundred and twenty full paid men. The department owns its own houses, numbering eighteen in all, each conforming in architecture to the locality in which it is located, all being thoroughly equipped with the latest modern appliances, to enable the men to make quick response to all alarms. There are one hundred and ninety-four street boxes, of the latest Gamewell pattern, with glass key protectors, enabling the citizen to ring an alarm without the least delay. Throughout the city are scattered six hundred and sixty hydrants, a great many in the business portion having double outlets. The Los Angeles Fire Department is up-to-date and will compare favorably with any department in cities of its size throughout the world, and is so recognized by the National Board of Underwriters. https://www.lafire.com/stations/LAFD-1900.htm

76 Engine 23 May 15 1915   Los Angeles, CA photo courtesy: LAFire.com, https://abandonedexplorers.com/ghostbusters-firehouse/

77 Engine 23 circa 1960 Los Angeles, CA photo courtesy: LAFire.com, https://abandonedexplorers.com/ghostbusters-firehouse/

78 With fireman Al Lambla at the reins, a turn of the century horsedrawn steamer races to a fire. Highlights in the history of the San Diego Fire Department—an agency that has now served San Diego for one hundred years. https://sandiegohistory.org/journal/1989/april/eating/

79 Firemen readying the horses at Fire Company No. 1. San Diego Fire Department, https://sandiegohistory.org/journal/1989/april/eating/

80 Engine 23 May 15 1915   Los Angeles, CA photo courtesy: LAFire.com

81 Fireman on house watch, 1906. https://www.nyhistory.org/blogs/what-the-business-requires-images

82 Fire Chief Edward F. Croker and opera singer Madam Nellie Melba inspecting Engine Co. 65, 1910. PR63. https://www.nyhistory.org/blogs/what-the-business-requires-images

83 In 1860, the city of Detroit purchased its first steam-powered firefighting equipment. It had a pumping capacity of 600 gallons a minute and was pulled to fires by two horses. Records show it cost $3,150. This steam engine is shown in an undated photo. THE DETROIT NEWS ARCHIVES https://www.detroitnews.com/picture-gallery/news/local/michigan-history/2015/08/23/detroit-firefighting-through-the-years/32034313/

84 Men with two fire engines in foreground and men fighting fire in background. Chicago : Published by E.W. Kelley, c1902. https://www.loc.gov/resource/cph.3b41776/

85 Engine 5 at 1906 Manhattan Ribbon Fire - On Arch Street bridge. https://www.patersonfirehistory.com/horse-drawn-apparatus.html

86 El Paso, Texas Hook & Ladder Truck No. 1 Horse Drawn Fire Engine. https://www.icollector.com/El-Paso-Texas-Hook-Ladder-Truck-No-1-Horse-Drawn-Fire-Engine-Real-Photo-Postcard_i40481331

87 Boys race to follow old-time horse-drawn fire engine to a fire. Clouds of coal smoke fly up from the steam boiler. Regular issue for June 29, 1911 of The Youth's Companion. https://archive.org/details/YouthsCompanion19110609

88 Photograph shows firemen riding horse-drawn steam powered fire engine down city street; crowds gather to watch. c1913. Wisconsin--Wausau. https://www.loc.gov/resource/cph.3a18877/

89 Fire horses in action, Winthrop, MA. c. 1917–1934. https://www.digitalcommonwealth.org/search/commonwealth:05742742x

90 The last of the Horses Engine Co. 205, New York Fire Department. c. 1922 Dec. 27. https://www.loc.gov/item/2005689017/

91 Horse-drawn fire engines in street, on their way to the Triangle Shirtwaist Company fire, New York City, 1911 March 25. https://www.loc.gov/item/2002709198/

92 Hose 5 on runners, West Newton, Feb 7, 1920.

93 Engine 22's horse-drawn steam pumper in the South End, circa 1900.

94 Horse drawn fire vehicle at intersection of West 43rd Street and Broadway, New York City. (Source: Flickr Commons project, 2010) [between ca. 1910 and ca. 1915] https://www.loc.gov/

item/2014695037/

95 Horse Drawn Steam Pumper Accident. Laurium MI, June 1, 1928

96 "Most of the streets were unpaved, making it easier for the horses to get a footing. On pavement the animals were likely to fall on turns. They did fall and tip the engine over at Fourth and C sts." — Clarence Woodson. [1913]. https://sandiegohistory.org/journal/1989/april/eating/

97 Fire equipment drawn by three running horses] circa. 1905 Nov. 16. https://www.loc.gov/item/2005689018/

98 Horse-Drawn Chief's Buggy, Shown here with Assistant Chief of Department - Ralph Cook, Photo taken: 1900 at Station 2 - 3rd Ave & Pine St. http://www.lastresortfd.org/SFD_History.htm#Chiefs%20Buggies

99 Chief John Stagg and driver George Pfitzenmeier in their gig in front of the 10 Hotel Street (Later renamed Hamilton Street) Headquarters (early 1900 photo). Notice Dietz Fire King Lantern at rear. Paterson Fire Department, New Jersey. https://www.patersonfirehistory.com/chief-gigs.html

100 The team pulling the ladder wagon waiting calmly. Working Horses : Looking Back 100 Years to America's Horse-Drawn Days by Charles Philip Fox (1990). National Sporting Library & Museum, the gift of The Little River Foundation. https://nslmblog.wordpress.com/2018/10/30/fire-horses/

101 Fire at close range, Whart St. Boston, MA. 1916. https://www.digitalcommonwealth.org/search/commonwealth:05742c54j

102 Horses protected with blankets at a fire. http://www.lastresortfd.org/SFD_History.htm#Chiefs%20Buggies

101 Jiggs, the long-time coach dog and mascot of Engine Company No. 205, howled in sorrow as his horse friends were bid their final farewell. https://www.patersonfirehistory.com/horse-drawn-apparatus.html

102 Fire department mascot Bozo gets a hug from Frank Noonan on May 24, 1929. Dog mascots were banned in 1976, over concerns that they might frighten citizens and prompt lawsuits. DETROIT NEWS PHOTO ARCHIVE https://www.detroitnews.com/picture-gallery/news/local/michigan-history/2015/08/23/detroit-firefighting-through-the-years/32034313/

103 Fire men and fire dogs https://www.digitalcommonwealth.org/search/commonwealth:5h73wf98w

104 First Bay Saranac Lake Firehouse https://www.saranaclakefire.com/content/history/

105 Interior of Gansevoort Street High Pressure Pumping Station, 1910. PR 63 https://www.nyhistory.org/blogs/what-the-business-requires-images

106 High-Pressure Pumping System test, West & Bank Streets, 1908. PR 63 https://www.nyhistory.org/blogs/what-the-business-requires-images

107 Paterson, New Jersey Fire Department with horses and walking horses

108 H Heinzelman, C Kennedy, J Eagan, Wm Smith , and horses of Engine Company 4 Circa 1911-12. https://www.patersonfirehistory.com/horse-drawn-apparatus.html

109 Steam Fire Engine No. 8, 1909. With snow on the ground Steamer No. 8, identified by the 8 near the rear, was one of the fire departments fighting a fire at the Burdick House, an hotel in Kalamazoo, on December 9, 1909. The steamer belonged Engine Company #8 of the Grand Rapids Fire Department, located at the corner of Jefferson St. (now Lexington) and Veto on the West Side. Three observers, including two youngsters, stand in the foreground. The Kalamazoo Gazette reported that the temperature that night was near zero. Grand Rapids Fire Department. Kalamazoo, MI. http://www.historygrandrapids.org/photo/4315/steam-fire-engine-no-8

110 In Canton, Massachusetts there are five firefighters standing around a hose wagon pulled by a horse. Two of the firefighters sit in the driver's seat and two on the back of the wagon. Another firefighter stands at the front of the horse in a suit and fire hat. https://www.digitalcommonwealth.org/search/commonwealth-oai:nv935p17w and https://www.historicnewengland.org/explore/collections-access/gusn/179689/

111 Three horse ladder truck. Lima Fire Department, Ohio

112 Armstrong 1890-12 Moustached man posed in studio in Fire Department uniform. Printed on card front: "McMichael, 210 & 212 Woodward Ave., Detroit." Printed on card back: "McMichael's photographic studio, Detroit, Mich. Duplicates and enlargements can be obtained at any time." Handwritten on card back: "A. Armstrong, December 1890. Supt. of horses." 1890 Detroit City Directory gives name as Allan Armstrong, superintendent

of horses for Fire Department. https://digitalcollections.detroitpubliclibrary.org/islandora/object/islandora%3A147629

113 Chief Martin Cooney, Supt. of Horses c.1880. Sepia-toned photo showing the head and shoulders of a fireman in a dress uniform. The photo is oval-shaped and is mounted on cardboard that has been cut out from a larger piece of mounting cardboard. Handwriting on the verso shows "Mr. McLaughlin, Asst. to Chief Martin Cooney, Supt. of Horses." http://detroithistorical.pastperfectonline.com/Photo/9EC66E56-43AE-471F-A849-944261241751

114 Sepia-toned photographic print of a group of nine firefighters of Chemical Company No. 6 posing with their horse-drawn fire engine in front of their fire house at Elmwood and Fort Street. The foremost driver is Martin Cooney, who would later become superintendent of horses, 1891. https://detroithistorical.pastperfectonline.com/Photo/86EC3AFA-90B7-4F76-A257-900459426986

115 Man and woman seated in horse-drawn buggy. Handwritten on back: "Allan Armstrong, supt of horses, DFD."

116 Sepia-toned photo showing an older fireman in uniform who is holding the bridle of a horse. A handwritten note across the top of the image shows "Martin Cooney, Supt. Horses, D.F.D." and horse. Building doorways (possibly for a horse stable) are visible in the background. c. 1910. http://detroithistorical.pastperfectonline.com/Photo/08BCB6AF-FA9E-4B61-BCE9-705448217534

117 Detroit Fire Department engine house (Engine Company 4) on Orchard and Fifth. 1881. Small plain brick building. Handwritten on back: "Fire engine house, Orchard & Fifth, 1881; Orchard now Elizabeth, Engine 4 built February 1865." https://digitalcollections.detroitpubliclibrary.org/islandora/object/islandora%3A147538 and https://detroit.fdmaps.com/engine-4/

118 Detroit Fire Department engine house (Engine Company 5) on Alexandrine near Cass, built in 1876. Small building with tall watchtower. Handwritten on back: "Engine house 1881, Alexandrine Ave. near Cass; see Farmer, Silas, History of Detroit, v. 1, p. 516; Engine 5 built June 1877." https://digitalcollections.detroitpubliclibrary.org//islandora/object/islandora:148298 and https://detroit.fdmaps.com/engine-5/

119 Detroit Firemen, 1890s. Sepia-toned photograph of two uniformed firefighters posed between three horses, which they are holding by the bit rings outside of the doorway of a brick stable. http://detroithistorical.pastperfectonline.com/Photo/6C2BE6DD-1702-408A-8DEC-724679131729

120 Excercisng horses attached to a skeleton wagon. c. 1902. Black and white photo of two firemen who are seated on a small wagon that is being drawn by three horses. Several brick and wood frame residential houses are visible in the background. Handwriting on the verso shows "D.F.D. approx. 1902. Eng. 9 exercise wagon shown with the steamer horses. If a fire company had no runs within a 24 hour period, the horses were exercised in local streets near the station houses. In the event of a fire, they would be notified to return to the station by ringing the tower bell." http://detroithistorical.pastperfectonline.com/Photo/1FFB14BA-1B11-4B2D-B65C-314287455501

121 Detroit Fire department horses starting a lesson, 1912. Detroit Historical Society. Postcard. Sepia-toned photographic postcard of a fireman holding two horses in front of station. A horse-drawn fire engine is barely visible beyond the doors in the background. Very tiny print in the lower left corner says "By C.A. Telfer, 1912." https://detroithistorical.pastperfectonline.com/Archive/CCC7B7DB-70C3-4C87-8C62-104010095220

122 One of Martin Coney's legers held by the Detroit Historical Society.

123 Auction Day at the great horse market, Detroit, Mich. Detroit Historical Society.

124 Mack served the Rescue firemen faithfully in York, Pennsylvania for 25 years. Photos courtesy of Detroit Historical Society, DFD Legacy and http://www.detroit.fdmaps.com/ Obituary Photo of "Mack" the 32-Year-Old, Veteran Hose Carriage Horse of Rescue Fire Company in York, PA (The York Daily, Dec. 4, 1911, Page 3) https://yorkblog.com/yorkspast/exploits-mack/ or https://www.roadsideamerica.com/tip/51236

125 Grave of Mack, Noble Fire Horse - Easy to find. Located on the corner next to the Fire House Museum. A five-foot-tall tombstone, complete with a chiseled horse's head, marks the grave of "noble horse" Mack, who died in 1911. At first he was buried in the woods, but he was later dug up, and he and his tombstone were moved next to the county fire museum. [Terry, 10/05/2018]

126 The first fire company in the City of Des Moines was organized in 1865, and was known as the "Hook & Ladder." After the City purchased an engine, the Company was reorganized under the name of the "Hawkeye Hose Company", with Charley Spofford as Chief Engineer. https://www.dsm.city/

departments/fire/fdhistory.php

127 Firehorse Fred died 1925. Fire Horse Fred pulled the New Bern fire hose wagon from 1908 to 1925. Endemic with so many heroic pets and animals, Fred was beloved by the firemen and the townspeople. He died in the harness pulling the crew to a false alarm. In gratitude, the men of Atlantic Company had Fred's head stuffed, and put in the Fireman's Museum when it was built in 1957. Fred's head is still on exhibit, stuffed and mounted in its own handsome display case. There's nothing much else here -- some vintage firetrucks, wagons, and old Pepsi bottles. https://www.newbernfiremuseum.com/ or https://www.roadsideamerica.com/story/2149

128 Chubby with fireman Frank Kalb. https://equitrekking.com/articles/entry/famous_horses_in_history_-_the_fire_horse

129 Obituary for the popular retired fire horse Chubby. From "Firefighter Chubby" on the Craft Company No. 6 site. https://nslmblog.wordpress.com/2018/10/30/fire-horses/

130 Bill and Chubby - Engine Company No. 6, Rochester, New York and Chubby. Craft Company No. 6. https://equitrekking.com/articles/entry/famous_horses_in_history_-_the_fire_horse

131 Kansas city fire horses - Having competed in the International Fire Congress competition in England in 1893, they won the Gold Medal for their innovative firefighting abilities under the command of long-time Fire Chief George Hale. The team, along with fire horses "Dan" and "Joe," also won first place awards in the hitching competition – reaching the scene and throwing water all in an elapsed time of 8.5 seconds. http://northeastnews.net/pages/fire-department-has-storied-history/

132 George C. Hale in Kansas City, http://atthefair.homestead.com/pkeatt/Halesfirefighter.html

133 Chief Edward Croker and bullet, http://hatchingcatnyc.com/2015/06/10/john-rush-victor-fire-horse-varick-street/ Chief Edward Croker (white hat) and his driver John Rush sometime in the early 1900s – I believe the horse in this photo was named Bullet. By this time chiefs in the FDNY were using automobiles to respond to fires, but a few horse-drawn buggies were kept in reserve because motorized vehicles were not always reliable. New York City Fire Museum Collections

134 Chief Edward Croker - Photographic print featuring Chief of Department Edward Croker and his driver in Croker's 1901 steam-driven buggy, the Locomobile. https://nycfiremuseum.pastperfectonline.com/photo/CD0167F9-D3D4-4267-8200-875056108855

135 Richmond Fire Department hose House No. 1 horses and firemen from early in the 20th c., stand proudly at what is now the site of the Firehouse BBQ & Blues at 400 North Eight & D Street. https://www.pal-item.com/story/news/local/2017/06/18/out-our-past-fire-department-used-rely-4-legged-heroes/405104001/

136 Proud steeds and crew at Richmond Fire Dept. Hose House No. 4. This structure at the southwest corner of South Ninth and E street still exists. Following is William R. Emslie's sketch of early Richmond fire department steeds. https://www.pal-item.com/story/news/local/2017/06/18/out-our-past-fire-department-used-rely-4-legged-heroes/405104001/

137 Horse no 12 - Gift of the District of Columbia Fire Department, 1902. Photo by Richard W. Strauss. Cauterized and preserved with a coat of shiny black enamel, the hoof of Horse No. 12 lived on as a memorial in the District of Columbia Fire Department. The Smithsonian exhibited the hoof as a loan, and later accepted it as a gift through the department's chief engineer, R. W. Dutton. Its placement in the National Museum, Dutton hoped, would "perpetuate the memory of an animal whose bravery and devotion to duty placed him high upon the department roll of honor." https://americanhistory.si.edu/blog/hoof-fire-horse-number-12

138 2 NE 82nd Avenue, Engine 27, 1913 - 1953, Montaville Neighborhood/Portland, Oregon https://www.portlandoregon.gov/fire/article/127248 The Kenton Firehouse, dedicated in 1913, was the first city-built station in North Portland. The facility, with its distinctive Second Renaissance Revival architecture, was built on land donated by a subsidiary of the Swift Meat Company. The main room once housed the hose wagon; the horses were stabled in what is the kitchen. Firemen lived upstairs where the North Portland Neighborhood Services office is now located. Used by the city until 1959, the Firehouse was designated a historical landmark in 1976 and given by the city into the care of neighborhood volunteers in 1977. The Firehouse has been a catalyst for public and private improvements in the neighborhood, and is used for family, community and business gatherings. All proceeds from rental of the facility are used by the volunteers of the Historic Kenton Firehouse Committee to maintain and restore this historic treasure. http://historickentonfirehouse.com/wp-content/uploads/2018/09/hkfh-flyer-2018.doc.pdf

139 Fire Station 2, at 510 NW Third Avenue, was in service from 1912 to 1950,fire station near

Northwest 3rd Avenue and Glisan https://www.portlandoregon.gov/fire/article/127334

140 *Painting of Jim the Fire Horse - After 25 years of searching, Mike Tressler, writer for the Toledo Blade, and Toledo Fire Department historian, Bill O'Connor, have located the famous painting of Jim the Fire Horse. "We received an e-mail recently from Mrs. Molly Cowan, Sylvania, OH, who inherited the portrait from her mother." The painting has been in her family for many years, originally having belonged to her grandfather, Harry J. Smith. Jim's portrait has lovingly hung in Mrs. Cowan's home and someday may eventually find itself at home in the museum in the special stall reserved for him.* https://www.merrimacknh.gov/about-fire-rescue/pages/horses-in-fire-service

141 *Painting of Jim the Fire Horse - After 25 years of searching, Mike Tressler, writer for the Toledo Blade, and Toledo Fire Department historian, Bill O'Connor, have located the famous painting of Jim the Fire Horse. "We received an e-mail recently from Mrs. Molly Cowan, Sylvania, OH, who inherited the portrait from her mother." The painting has been in her family for many years, originally having belonged to her grandfather, Harry J. Smith. Jim's portrait has lovingly hung in Mrs. Cowan's home and someday may eventually find itself at home in the museum in the special stall reserved for him.* https://www.merrimacknh.gov/about-fire-rescue/pages/horses-in-fire-service

142 *Funeral procession for Jim the fire horse.* https://www.merrimacknh.gov/about-fire-rescue/pages/horses-in-fire-service

143 *Johnson, Herbert, 1878-1946, artist. c1922.* https://www.loc.gov/resource/acd.2a09427/ or https://www.loc.gov/item/2016682157/

144 *The Rochester American Legion created a bronze plaque in 1926 that still stands today and fittingly describes all fire horses.* https://equitrekking.com/articles/entry/famous_horses_in_history_-_the_fire_horse

145 *Lt. Loebel with neighbor boy back of Engine House 12.* http://lafire.com/stations/era-of-horses-index.htm

146 *Young boy Frankie Williams with "Dimple," fire department horse, Seattle, 1922. The Seattle Fire Department held a parade down 2nd Avenue in November 1922 as part of a farewell to veteran horses like "Dimple," shown here with a little boy outside Station 35. In June 1924, it was announced in the Seattle Times that all fire horses would be retired.* https://digitalcollections.lib.washington.edu/digital/collection/imlsmohai/id/1753/ *Photographer, Webster & Stevens.*

147 *The Cleveland Fire Department's Engine NO. 2 on Public Square, ca. 1910. WRHS.* https://case.edu/ech/articles/c/cleveland-fire-department

148 *LA fire horse running - Three muscular horses pull a Los Angeles fire engine up a First Street Hill, circa 1900. Courtesy of the USC Libraries - California Historical Society Collection.* https://waterandpower.org/museum/Early_City_Views%20%281900%20-%201925%29_1_of_8.html *This photo was published in the Jan. 3, 1950, Los Angeles Times Mid-Winter Edition as part of a photographic history of Los Angeles. The accompanied headline announced, "Century's Early Years Brought Trolleys, Traffic and (Ah!) Fashion." *## (ca.1900)^^ - View showing an early fire engine pulled by large muscular horses, up a hill on First Street. Several firefighters help push the fire engine as it makes its way up the hill. The horses kick up a lot of dirt and dust as it pulls the long fire engine. On the fire engine, there is one driver who steers the horses in the front of the engine, and there is one driver in the rear who appears to be holding onto a steering wheel. A large shiny bell is mounted on the engine in front of the firefighter steering the horses. A large ladder, attached to the fire engine, can be seen along the body of the vehicle. The dirt road is littered with rocks. At left, about five children can be seen playing on the sidewalk or looking at the commotion. A woman can be seen in her window in the two-story house at left. Caption reads: "Early days with the fire companies. A hard pull up First Street hill toward a fire."*

149 *Fire Station Portrait with Curious Children. Photo Care of: Kentucky Library and Museum, Western Kentucky University. During the 1870's, 80's and 90's, various purchases were made to add to and repair the fire apparatus for the volunteers. On September 1, 1898, Bowling Green's first paid fire department came into existence. John Moltenberry and Dave W. Harrison were appointed firemen, since both had seen action as volunteers. The chief of the department was James A. Wilkerson, who also served as the city engineer at the same time and had been chief of the volunteer department.* https://www.bgky.org/history/photo-gallery or https://www.bgky.org/history/fire

150 *Bowling Green Fire Department Horse and Buggy Parade. Photo Care of: Kentucky Library and Museum, Western Kentucky University. As the department became a paid one, it also moved its*

headquarters to a new location on State Street. In addition, the firefighters could ride on a hose and chemical wagon pulled by a team of horses rather than having to pull their equipment to a fire by hand. Hose and chemical wagons were purchased in 1898 and 1900, while a hook and ladder was purchased in 1901. Until the early 1900's when the paid department was enlarged, the volunteers aided the paid firefighters by running to the fire station and pulling their hose reels to the fire scene in order to assist. Around this same time, 17 fire alarm boxes were placed in the business section of Bowling Green and were abandoned for use when telephones became available. In April of 1904, John Moltenberry was appointed to the position of chief after having spent 2 years as a firefighter and 3 years as a captain. Moltenberry served as chief until the end of 1938. His tenure as the city's first full-time paid fire chief saw many changes and improvements in the department. A new central fire station was completed in 1909 at a cost of about $10,000. In January of 1912, the chief's pay was $85 per month, captains received $65 and firefighters with more than two years of experience received $60. Lesser experienced firefighters received less pay. The department at that time consisted of ten men that worked six days and six nights and had one day off. In 1914, a "motor hose & chemical wagon" was purchased and by 1918, horse drawn fire engines had been totally eliminated. Chief Moltenberry apparently was in favor of replacing the horses because they "were always getting sick." https://www.bgky.org/history/fire

151 Prince and Paddy https://siouxcityjournal.com/blogs/siouxland_history/50-years-ago-sioux-city-author-writes-children-s-book-about-prince-and-paddy/article_659907d8-7d3b-51d7-8928-759a345e8e9d.html

152 Fourth of July early 1900's--Horse-Drawn Fire Wagon #1 (in front of the new Victor City Hall constructed after the Great Fire of August 1899) is decorated for the parade. According to the caption embedded at the top of the photo, "the following year, the Victor Fire Department won the World Hose Run Championship in San Francisco." Read Gertrudes's account of the day of the parade, https://www.victorheritagesociety.com/gold-camp-celebration--fourth-of-july-in-victor-early-1900s-by-gertrude-moore-mcgowan.html

153 Hale's Firefighters, 1893 - a 5,000 seat auditorium for the 50 minute show. repeated four times daily. The show began with informative on how the fire wagons worked as well as draft horses leaping through `fire.' Then the set switched to a New York City street and illustrated how the brave firefighters were alerted, responded and dealt with a six-story building fire. There were women and children to rescued, while hoses were fighting the `blaze,' the strongest men pumped the `water.' http://atthefair.homestead.com/pkeatt/Halesfirefighter.html

154 Hale Firefighters' celebrated Pompier Life-saving Corps. The members of this corps are Captain Al Graefer, Adolph Graefer, Henry Schaffnit, Irs Jackson, Frederick Wilson, William McCornwell, George Phipps and Sylvester Ingram. https://thumbs.worthpoint.com/zoom/images3/1/0712/08/hales-fire-fighters-exhibition_1_f246633060d40f0d4a3cf0a0e53b52ef.jpg

155 Souvenir, Hale's Fire Fighters, World's Fair Saint Louis, 1904. https://www.worthpoint.com/worthopedia/hales-fire-fighters-exhibition-19681223

156 This photo shows a horse-drawn fire wagon running on Westport Road near Pennsylvania Avenue in preparation for the fire department's trip to Paris in 1900. Fire department horses were revered by the firefighters who trained and cared for them. Having competed in the International Fire Congress competition in England in 1893, they won the Gold Medal for their innovative firefighting abilities under the command of long-time Fire Chief George Hale. The team, along with fire horses "Dan" and "Joe," also won first place awards in the hitching competition – reaching the scene and throwing water all in an elapsed time of 8.5 sec. Read more at: https://www.kansascity.com/news/local/article59303278.html#storylink=cpy

157 Published in the The New York Times, Sunday, February 19, 1911. https://blogs.microsoft.com/wp-content/uploads/prod/sites/154/2018/01/horse_newspaper.jpg or https://blogs.microsoft.com/today-in-tech/day-horse-lost-job/

158 Fire horses leave the quarters of FDNY Engine 39 and Ladder 16 on East 67th Street for the last time in 1911. Their replacement: the first gasoline-powered pumper, seen in the background. Photo, Library of Congress. https://hatchingcatnyc.com/2015/02/01/upstate-city-farm-retired-fire-horses/

159 George W. Murray drives Balgriffen, Danny Beg, and Penrose on the final call for the last-horse-drawn engine in FDNY history. On the ash pan behind, Captain Leon Howard was keeping his hand on the whistle rope so that it screamed one long blast; Engineer Tom McEwen pushed coal into the firebox with both feet and one hand (he used his other hand to hold on tight). http://hatchingcatnyc.com/2015/01/24/last-fire-horses-new-york-fire-department/

160 A San Francisco Fire Department boiler rig and team in action. The boiler produced steam, which created a vacuum in the 2,000-pound steamer and enabled firemen to suck water from a reservoir or other source through the steamer to be shot up under pressure into the fire hoses. This enabled firemen to fight multi-story fires from the street for the first time. The horse teams were incredibly well trained and disciplined. Each fireman was assigned one horse to care for and the bonds between them were deep. Martin Murry Dunn was known throughout the Bay Area for breeding fine fire horses. Image from the book "Eccentrics, Heroes, and Cutthroats" by Richard Schwartz.Courtesy Richard Schwartz. By the early 1910s, San Francisco firefighters were ready. https://www.sfchronicle.com/oursf/article/Our-SF-Fire-horses-doomed-after-losing-6601116.php

161 Portland Engine 4, 1913. City of Portland Archives.

162 One of the city's last horse-drawn fire trucks on an alarm call, 1920, Chicago. " http://www.connectingthewindycity.com/2018/02/february-5-1923-last-run-for-fire-house.html

163 Displacing horse drawn for motor driven apparatus in the Quarters of Engine Company 21, 1152 Oak Street, San Francisco, CA. Sept. 19, 1915. Celebrating the move to motorized apparatus in 1915. https://hoodline.com/2016/04/inside-old-station-21-landmark-firehouse/The presence of this firehouse in the late 1800s and early 1900s also marked the transition from horse-drawn carriages to fire engine machines—or as some would say, from "analog to digital". The huge earthquake and subsequent fire of 1906 marked a time when the majority of San Francisco firehouses were still using horse-drawn carriages to get to the scene of a fire. Firehouse No. 21 spent the majority of that time valiantly fighting fires in Hayes Valley for a whopping 54 hours. We found an old log at the library describing Firehouse No. 21's experiences that day: "The reports written just after the 1906 fire are fearsome tales. Captain H. Boden wrote that because the alarm and telephone systems which were not in order after the earthquake, they proceeded eastward "where we observed a column of smoke". They fought fire after fire, mostly in the Hayes Valley, trying again and again to obtain water. They finally returned to their station at 11:30am on April 20th, "having been on duty for fifty four hours". Besides Captain Boden, James Feeny, M. J. O'Connor, P.J. Meehan, W. Leonhardt, E. Long, T. Meacham, D. O'Connell and Charles Tyson fought these fires.

164 Preparing for the last running of the Detroit Fire Horses. http://www.dfdlegacy.com/detroit-fire-department-history-last-running-of-the-fire-horses/

165 More than 50,000 people gathered to witness the historic last run or Peter, Jim, Tom, Babe and Rusty, the horses of Engine 37's steamer and hose wagons. They dashed down Woodward on a symbolic final emergency as a fake alarm sounded at the National Bank Building. http://www.dfdlegacy.com/detroit-fire-department-history-last-running-of-the-fire-horses/

167 Horse drawn fire wagon and the new-fangled variety in one shot. The horses look less than impressed. Harold Stanfield photo, MCHS

168 Cast-iron horse drawn steam engine and ladder truck from the Gloria Austin Colletion. Cast-iron toys, such as the fire engine from about 1900, reflect many commonplace but often forgotten aspects of everyday life. The strength of the Museum's toy collection is an outstanding grouping of cast-iron and tinplate toys, 1870s to the 1950s, donated by Sears, Roebuck and Co. The collection was acquired by Sears, Roebuck and Co. from Kenneth Idle, a private collector. Gathered between 1915 and 1960, the collection numbers more than 1,400 cast-iron and tinplate examples of both American and European origins. Cast-iron toy manufacturers represented in this collection are Hubley, Kentontoys, and Kingsbury Toys. Subjects include the circus, horse-drawn vehicles, public transportation, mail delivery, home equipment, recreation, construction equipment, the farm, fire fighting, and police vehicles. Cast-iron toys are essentially American. Small foundries and factories were mass-producing them towards the close of the 19th century. These toys were sold in novelty stores, department stores, or mail order catalogs. One can follow along with shifts in technology by recognizing the changes in the different models of Sears toys. During the first half of the 20th century, tractors almost completely displaced the horse on American farms—and on the toy counter. Toy motor trucks replaced horse-drawn vehicles. The toy manufacturers were alert to new models and designs of vehicle and appliance manufacturers. Cited: https://americanhistory.si.edu/collections/search/object/nmah_314550

169 Photograph by Everett.Firemen on Horse-Drawn Fire Truck, "On the Way to a Fire", Chicago, USA, Postcard, circa 1890. Photograph by Everett. http://www.chicagopostcardmuseum.org/i_will_gallery_series.html

170 587 BC – The destruction of the Temple and city of Jerusalem. By Internet Archive Book Images - https://www.flickr.com/photos/internetarchivebookimages/14783032815/Source book page: https://archive.org/stream/artbiblecomprisi00lond/artbiblecomprisi00lond#page/n907/mode/1up, No restrictions, https://commons.wikimedia.org/w/index.php?curid=44201898

171 - 64 – Great Fire of Rome, Italy. By Hubert Robert - http://www.kunst-fuer-alle.de/index.php?mid=77&lid=1&blink=76&stext=caesar&cmstitle=Bilder,-Kunstdrucke,-Poster:-Caesar&start=80, Public Domain, https://commons.wikimedia.org/w/index.php?curid=6606073

172 - 1204 – Sack of Constantinople (1204). Constantinople was burned three times during the Fourth Crusade. By David Aubert (1449-79) - 15th century miniature. [1] « Croniques abregies commençans au temps de Herode Antipas, persecuteur de la chrestienté, et finissant l'an de grace mil IIc et LXXVI », ou « livre traittant en brief des empereurs », par David Aubert. Tome II f 205r, Public Domain, https://commons.wikimedia.org/w/index.php?curid=3107592

173 - 532 – The Nika riots result in the destruction of much of Constantinople by fire. By Jean Le Tavernier - Illustration by fr (Jean Le Tavernier) accompanying a translation by Jean Miélot of Bertrandon de la Broquière's Voyage d'Outre-Mer. It is one of three full-page miniatures in the Bibliothèque nationale de France, MSS fr. 9087, at folio 207 vv.Image taken from:http://expositions.bnf.fr/flamands/grand/fla_444.htm, Public Domain, https://commons.wikimedia.org/w/index.php?curid=87115344

174 - 1204 – Sack of Constantinople (1204). Constantinople was burned three times during the Fourth Crusade. By David Aubert (1449-79) - 15th century miniature. [1] « Croniques abregies commençans au temps de Herode Antipas, persecuteur de la chrestienté, et finissant l'an de grace mil IIc et LXXVI », ou « livre traittant en brief des empereurs », par David Aubert. Tome II f 205r, Public Domain, https://commons.wikimedia.org/w/index.php?curid=3107592

175 - 1571 – The 1571 Moscow fire occurred when the forces of the Crimean khan Devlet I Giray raided the city. By anonimus - http://www.runivers.ru/bookreader/book482205/#page/17/mode/1up, Public Domain, https://commons.wikimedia.org/w/index.php?curid=42008545

176 - 1666 – Great Fire of London. Read Samuel Pepys diary entry on London fire, Sunday, Sept 2, 1666. https://www.pepysdiary.com/diary/1666/09/02/. If you read on, you will learn there are many stories for how the fire was started. Robert Hubert - frenchman said to start fire, plus other thoeories https://www.pepysdiary.com/encyclopedia/10872/ Samuel Pepys entry - https://www.pepysdiary.com/diary/1667/02/24/ Popish plot to kill the king (1666-79) pg233-36 of History of England from the Accession of James II, Vol I by Thomas Babington Macaulay, Hannah Trevelyan (1850) London: Longman, Brown, Green, Longmans, and Roberts. In 1986, London's bakers finally apologized to the lord mayor for setting fire to the city. Members of the Worshipful Company of Bakers gathered on Pudding Lane and unveiled a plaque acknowledging that one of their own, Thomas Farrinor, was guilty of causing the Great Fire of 1666. https://www.history.com/this-day-in-history/great-fire-of-london-begins / Cestui Que Vie Act 1666 https://www.legislation.gov.uk/aep/Cha2/18-19/11 An Act for Redresse of Inconveniencies by want of Proofe of the Deceases of Persons beyond the Seas or absenting themselves, upon whose Lives Estates doe depend. X1Recital that Cestui que vies have gone beyond Sea, and that Reversioners cannot find out whether they are alive or dead. [I.]Cestui que vie remaining beyond Sea for Seven Years together and no Proof of their Lives, Judge in Action to direct a Verdict as though Cestui que vie were dead. IVIf the supposed dead Man prove to be alive, then the Title is revested. Action for mean Profits with Interest. When London burned, the subrogation of men's and women's rights occurred. The responsible act passed… CQV act 1666 meant all men and women of UK were declared dead and lost beyond the seas. The state took everybody and everybody's property into trust. The state takes control until a living man or woman comes back and claims their titles by proving they are alive and claims for damages can be made. This is why you always need representation

177 - 1676 – Jamestown, Virginia was burned by Nathaniel Bacon and his followers during Bacon's Rebellion to prevent Governor Berkley from using it as a base. By Robert Sears, A pictorial description of the United States (s.n., 1854), pg. 315 https://books.google.com/books?id=sfKAAAAAIAAJ&source=gbs_navlinks_s - Robert Sears, A pictorial description of the United States (s.n., 1854), pg. 315 https://books.google.com/books?id=sfKAAAAAIAAJ&source=gbs_navlinks_s, Public Domain, https://commons.wikimedia.org/w/index.php?curid=9008949

178 - 1702 – Uppsala, Sweden, devastated in large part and the cathedral and Uppsala Castle severely damaged. Ruins of Uppsala Castle's south wing and southeast tower following the fire of 1702. The drawing's title indicates parts of the ruined castle were under demolition at the time. The depiction shows that the western part of the south wing, which housed the royal apartments, had been razed (it would have been located in the left-most part of the drawing). The east wing, or "Long Castle," which mostly survived the fire is not shown (it would at the right-most part of the drawing). By Jean Eric Rehn - Nationalmuseum, NMH 1748/1875, Public Domain, https://commons.wikimedia.org/w/index.php?curid=110882235

179 - 1731 – Tiverton fire, Devon, England, burned nearly 300 houses. Rumored to start in a bakers house. Public Domain, https://commons.wikimedia.org/w/index.php?curid=1113069

180 - 1776 – First Great Fire of New York City of 1776. By Franz Xaver Habermann - New York Public Library Digital Collection: Image ID=psnypl_prn_972 URL: http://digitalgallery.nypl.org/nypldigital/id?psnypl_prn_972, Public Domain, https://commons.wikimedia.org/w/index.php?curid=2609949

181 - 1793 – Cap Français (modern-day Cap-Haïtien, Haiti). By J.-B. Chapuy, Graveur ; J.-L. Boquet, Peintre du modèle (Boquet, Pierre Jean L. 1751-1817 ?) - Bibliothèque nationale de France, Public Domain, https://commons.wikimedia.org/w/index.php?curid=12999214

182 - 1814 – Great fire of Tirschenreuth in Tirschenreuth, Bavaria, totally destroys the town apart from the parish church and 3 neighboring buildings. By Unknown author - Tirschenreuther Krippenbuch, Seite 21, Public Domain, https://commons.wikimedia.org/w/index.php?curid=7894005

183 - 1827 – Great Fire of Turku, Finland By Gustaf Wilhelm Finnberg - https://d3uvo7vkyyb63c.cloudfront.net/1/webp/4000/256385.jpg, Public Domain, https://commons.wikimedia.org/w/index.php?curid=4554666

184 - 1849 – St. Louis Fire of 1849, saw the first US firefighter killed in the line of duty. 1849 – First Gr. Ruins of the Great St. Louis Fire, 17-18 May 1849. Daguerreotype by Thomas M. Easterly, 1849. By Thomas Martin Easterly - Missouri History Museum Photographs and Prints Collections, Public Domain, https://commons.wikimedia.org/w/index.php?curid=11932899

185 - 1850 – Kraków Fire of 1850, Poland, affects 10% of the city area. The fire made the city government increase the fire fighting budget, though the first (voluntary) fire service would not be established until 1865. By Teodor Baltazar Stachowicz (1800-1873) - http://www.geo.uj.edu.pl/opracowania/historia/images/4_pier13.jpg, Public Domain, https://commons.wikimedia.org/w/index.php?curid=44082414

186 - 1866 – Great Portland Fire of 1866, Maine, destroyed the commercial district and left 10,000 homeless. Ruins of the Great Fire at Portland, Me. July 4th & 5th, 1866. -- View from Corner of Middle & Free Sts. By Joseph E. Baker (1837–1914), artist and lithographer; published by Bufford Brothers, Boston & New York - Transferred from en.wikipedia to Commons. (Original text : Collection of the Osher Map Library, University of Southern Maine, Portland, MaineSource site: http://www.usm.maine.edu/maps/Source URL: http://usm.maine.edu/maps/exhibition/13/5/%5Bfield_sub_section-raw%5D/48/j-e-baker-ruins-of-the-great-fire-at-portland-me), Public Domain, https://commons.wikimedia.org/w/index.php?curid=20252977

187 - 1871 – Great Chicago Fire of 1871 destroyed the downtown on October 8 and died out the following night. About 250 dead. The Currier & Ives lithograph shows people fleeing across the Randolph Street Bridge. By Currier and Ives - Chicago Historical Society (ICHi-23436), Public Domain, https://commons.wikimedia.org/w/index.php?curid=62278069

188 - 1872 – Great Boston Fire of 1872, destroyed 776 buildings and killed at least 20 people. Photograph of the ruins left by the Great Boston Fire in the downtown area. Took place November 1872. Public Domain, https://commons.wikimedia.org/w/index.php?curid=234668

189 - 1886 – Fire in Calgary, Alberta. Big fire on 9th Avenue SE, Calgary, Alberta. Big fire on 9th Avenue, Calgary, Alberta, between Centre Street and 1st Street SE. I.S. Freeze, J. Paterson, and Grand Central Hotel buildings in middleground. Contents of various buildings piled in foreground. By Ross, Alexander J. - This image is available from the Glenbow Museum under the reference number CU1115356 and under the University of Calgary Libraries and Cultural Resources Digital Collection Permanent link 2R3BF1OT23D6, Public Domain, https://commons.wikimedia.org/w/index.php?curid=87937641

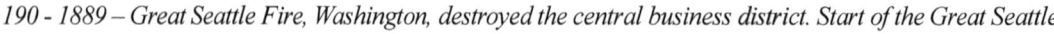

190 - 1889 – Great Seattle Fire, Washington, destroyed the central business district. Start of the Great Seattle

Fire of June 6, 1889, looking south on 1st Ave. near Madison St. By University of Washington Libraries Digital Collections, Public Domain, https://commons.wikimedia.org/w/index.php?curid=10552537

191 - 1892 – Great Fire of 1892 in St. John's, Newfoundland. St. John's, Newfoundland after the fire of 1892. By Unknown author - Provincial Archives of Newfoundland and Labrador, Public Domain, https://commons.wikimedia.org/w/index.php?curid=63801620

192 - 1906 – San Francisco earthquake and fire. By Internet Archive Book Images - https://www.flickr.com/photos/internetarchivebookimages/14764207244/Source book page: https://archive.org/stream/historyofearthqu00aitk/historyofearthqu00aitk#page/n115/mode/1up, No restrictions, https://commons.wikimedia.org/w/index.php?curid=43827011

193 - 1914 – Great Salem Fire of 1914, Massachusetts. Bird's-eye view of ruins of Great Salem Fire, June 25, 1914. By Unknown photographer - Reproduced from an original postcard published by Tichnor Brothers, Boston, Massachusetts, Public Domain, https://commons.wikimedia.org/w/index.php?curid=20250808

www.ingramcontent.com/pod-product-compliance
Lightning Source LLC
Chambersburg PA
CBHW050750110526
44592CB00002B/20